The Incredible Patience of God

Along the Road
to Spiritual Maturity

Lane Adams

PRESS

Originally published by Tyndale House Publishers, Inc.,
Wheaton, Illinois, as *How Come It's Taking Me So Long?*
Revised 1999.

The author gratefully acknowledges permission to quote
from the following versions of the Bible, in addition to the
King James Version:

The Living Bible
© 1971 by Tyndale House Publishers, Inc.,
Wheaton, Illinois.

The Holy Bible, New International Version
© 1973, 1978, 1984 by International Bible Society.
Used by permission of Zondervan Bible Publishers.
All Rights reserved.

The Modem Language Bible, The Berkeley Version
edited by Gerrit Verkuyl, Ph.D., © 1945, 1959,
© 1969 by the Zondervan Publishing House,

Grand Rapids, Michigan

The Revised Standard Edition
© 1946 and 1952, Division of Christian Education of
the National Council of the Churches of Christ in the
United States of America, New York, New York.

The New American Standard Bible
© 1960, 1962, 1963, 1968, 1971,
The Lockman Foundation, La Habra, California.

The New Testament in Modern English
by J. B. Phillips, © 1958, 1959, 1960 by J. B.
Phillips, The Macmillan Company,
New York, New York.

Note: The masculine pronoun is used in referring to a person of unknown gender in order to simplify the language.
the author in no way intends to imply any limitations or to
offend any reader.

Xulon Press
www.XulonPress.com

Xulon Press books are available in bookstores everywhere,
and on the Web at www.XulonPress.com.

To my wife
ANNETTE
*who has been
with me
in the maturing
process
over the years,
helping me
understand
the patience
of God*

CONTENTS

FOREWORD

I CAN REMEMBER the radiance I saw on his
face and the excitement he expressed. The man was
a seasoned Elder of our Hollywood Church.
He had given his life to Christ years before and
had struggled to grow to become a mature Christian.
Discouraging battles with his own humanity had
made the Christian life a disappointing experience
of ups and downs. Now he had found a liberating
secret which gave him hope. He had attended
Lane Adams's Inquirers' Group for prospective
members of our church. What Lane had shared had
given him an exuberant burst of enthusiasm
and freedom. He had gone to the classes as a dutiful
Elder to be supportive of our church's ministry of
evangelism. By the time the course was completed he
was not only evangelized himself, he was emancipated
from deadly dicta which had locked him on
dead center.

I will never forget what this Elder, a Christian
for twenty-three years, said to me. "Why did
I have to wait so long to discover what Lane taught
about the true nature of Christian growth? When
I think of all the years of anguishing trial and
error, I wish I had learned this twenty-three years ago.
Everyone's got to go to those classes!"

What this Elder heard from Lane is the essential
content of this exciting book you are about to read.
Each time we receive a group of new members,
I hear and see the implications of this same
inspiration expressed by this Elder. The Session
meets with these new members to affirm and
encourage their commitment to Christ and their
desire to grow in Christ by participation in the
adventuresome new chapter of the Book of Acts which
is being dramatized in our church. I am always

gratified by the authentic introduction to Christ
Lane has enabled in each of them. But my joy
overflows each time the new members talk about the
vision and vitality they have received about what
it means to grow to maturity in Christ. So many
of the hang-ups and false expectations which I find
in Christians all around the world have been
anticipated and alleviated in these new Christians

uniting with our church.

Lane Adams is obstetrician, pediatrician, and
internist when it comes to introducing people to Christ,
enabling their first stumbling steps of growth
and diagnosing and treating the complex problems
of being faithful and obedient to Christ as maturing
Christians. Few Christian leaders have all these
gifts. But Lane has exercised all of them in his
winsome leadership in our church and now in this
desperately needed book.

I remember when I first met this fellow-adventurer
face to face. We had agreed to meet in Denver
to talk about the possibility of teaming together.
There was that immediate koinonia which is
experienced by two brothers whose hearts feel the
drumbeat of the Master. The same openness,
vulnerability, and honest freedom you will feel on
every page of this book was what impressed me so
much at that first meeting. The usual tension of job
interviews was completely lacking as we shared
our lives with each other. Lane led not from
strength and adequacy but from weakness and a
voracious desire to grow in Christ. I have met few
people whose commitment to Christ was more
stable and yet whose openness about their own needs
was more viable.

It was at that meeting that I first heard the basic
thesis of this book. I had asked Lane what he

wanted to have happen to people through his
ministry. In response he outlined the undergirding
theory of his ministry of introducing people to the
Savior in such a way that they would be free to grow
and discover the amazing possibilities of Christ
liberated from the reservations and self-justifications
which debilitate so many defeated Christians. I
still remember the diagram of the invasion, beachhead,
and penetration of the enemy-held territory he
drew for me. From the experience he had had as a
navy pilot in World War II, he illustrated one of
the most vivid explanations of conversion and
sanctification I had ever heard. I know you
will feel the same way as you are drawn magnetically
on through the evolving discovery of this
thought-provoking book.

I have just finished reading the manuscript for
myself. I was personally helped and encouraged by it.
So many Christian writers have a way of taking the
dynamic of the gospel and complicating it
unnecessarily with restrictive rhetoric. Too seldom
do we feel the author's own experience of the
truth he is communicating. Not so with this book!
The thought is profound, but the joy and freedom
with which Lane writes pulls the reader on chapter to
chapter. This book is like a conversation. The
real man who wrote it sparkles through each page.
His rich humor, his extensive experience and
his Holy Spirit-inspired insights make this book
difficult to put down. There is a powerful use of
Scripture which reveals Lane's love and understanding
of the Bible. The deeply personal illustrations
help us to know that the author has lived what he
writes. The personal needs in his own life are
brewing beneath the surface of so many Christians.
This book answers the questions we are all

asking. There is nothing more absurd than an answer to an unasked question and nothing more powerful than the clear answer to the deepest questions in our hearts. Here is the answer to one of the most persistent questions I hear asked in so many ways by so many Christians. Lane is a man who has had the courage to say it as it is! I thank God for that.

We have needed this book for a long time but God's timing is always right. There has never been a greater need than now.

I pray that this book will mean to you as much as its author has come to mean to me and our church in Hollywood.

LLOYD JOHN OGILVIE, 1975
Then Pastor,
The First Presbyterian Church
of Hollywood
Currently Chaplain,
United States Senate

"OH! THAT DOES MAKE ME FEEL much
better about a lot of things!"

A young lady said that to me just after I had briefly
reviewed for her the major ideas of this book.
I turned to Virginia Muir, Tyndale House's senior
book editor, who was seated at the same luncheon
table, and said, "If the book brings that kind of
response from its readers, it will have accomplished the
purpose for which it was written."

The young lady who had given the positive
response was a Christian worker who had returned
from an overseas mission field and was presently
engaged in a professional position not related
to institutional Christianity. Happy with her new
vocation, she was obviously still working through the
personal needs which had necessitated her return.

The purpose of this book is to bring comfort
and understanding to all who name Jesus as Lord and
Savior. I pray that its message will free many
believers to patiently enjoy the maturing process
as God is working in their lives. It is designed to
bring a fresh biblical understanding of conversion and
growth, and thereby to bring relief to the person
who keeps wondering, "How come it's taking me
so long to get better?" Since this book concerns
the passage of time, it might be well to point out that
the struggles described here cover a span of
more than twenty-five years.

In today's religious climate, there is a real danger
in publishing a book under the title *The Incredible
Patience of God*. The current imbalance in
understanding tends towards a warped view of God
that almost turns him into a wimp. God is pictured as
willing to forgive anything, anytime, regardless of
how long one persists in the sin.

A friend was counseling a woman who came to her after our friend spoke at a church. It was a church noted for the "experiences" they offered their worshipers. This young woman already had one child born out of wedlock. Although I do not know exactly what was distressing her, she, incredibly, suggested that perhaps it would help her situation if she had another baby out of wedlock. Shocked, our friend pointed out that such a thing would be sinful, and was a direct violation of the seventh commandment, which prohibits sex outside of marriage. To this, the young woman airily responded, "So? God will forgive me!" To such a flippant response, reflecting "cheap grace," our Lord Jesus warns: "Not everyone who says to me, 'Lord, Lord,' will enter the kingdom of heaven, but only he who does the will of my Father who is in heaven. Many will say to me on that day, 'Lord, Lord, did we not . . . drive out demons and perform many miracles?' Then I will tell them plainly, 'I never knew you. Away from me, you evildoers!'" [literally, "lawless"] (Matthew 7:21-23, NIV).

In 1973 when I joined Lloyd John Ogilvie in his God-blessed ministry at the famed Hollywood Presbyterian Church, I asked him what he thought the number one problem was in and out of the church there in California. In a flash he responded, "Antinomianism!" That big theological word is easy to understand. "Anti" means "against," and "nomos" is the Greek word for "law." It means people who are either "against" the law of God, "lawless," or who are totally "indifferent" to it. In his preaching, Lloyd rarely raised that magnificent, deep, "canyon-shaped" voice of his. But on one occasion in 1990, I heard him boom out to the packed sanctuary, and beyond to the television and radio audience, "If any of you are breaking any one of the Ten Commandments, I am telling you to STOP IT! STOP IT RIGHT NOW!" He then explained how destructive such behavior was both to the perpetrator and to society. Throughout the 17 years of his ministry there, he had his eye on the target. (Dr. Ogilvie is now chaplain to the United States Senate.)

The person who is experiencing the saving work of the living Christ in his life hates the snail-like pace of the maturing process. He hurts inside when he knows that he is displeasing his Savior either with his inner attitude or his outward behavior. We use a playpen to limit how far a baby or toddler can crawl or walk. Many in the church suffer from "playpen theology." They are constantly seeing how far they can go before they are displeasing to God. The person in whom the Savior is working begins his day asking, "Lord, what can I do today to bring glory and honor to Your Name?" rather than, "How far can I go and still get away with it?"

The purpose of what I have written is to let the Bible speak for itself in instructing us what to expect regarding the maturing process. God forbid that it should be used to play fast and loose with the "incredible patience of God." As the Book of Hebrews says, "We must pay more careful attention, therefore, to what we have heard, so that we do not drift away. For if the message spoken by angels was binding, and every violation and disobedience received its just punishment, how shall we escape if we ignore such a great salvation?" (Hebrews 2:1–3, NIV).

As in most things, balance is what we seek to achieve in this long process of spiritual maturation. Paul wrote to the Roman Christians, "Consider therefore the kindness and sternness of God: sternness to those who fell, but kindness to you, provided that you continue in his kindness. Otherwise, you also will be cut off" (Romans 11:22, NIV).

I wish to acknowledge with gratitude the editorial assistance of my son-in-law, Terry Moore, and the exceptionally patient and encouraging secretarial assistance of Belva Jean Russell. Also, a hearty thanks to volunteer typists Deena Putnam, Peggy Duarte, Barbara Kefauver, and Joyce Nelson, who spent much time transcribing tapes.

I want to especially thank the Coastline Community Church of Solona Beach, California, and its pastor, James Christoferson, for having the faith to give me a magnificent computer that has aided immensely in producing this book.

LANE G. ADAMS

Editor's Note: Although the author is allegedly retired, he continues an active speaking ministry as the voluntary Minister-At-Large for the Plymouth Rock Foundation. This ministry is dedicated to reminding America about the biblical roots implanted in this nation by its founders, and of the danger of departing from those foundations. For more information on this ministry, contact the author at the following address:

Dr. Lane G. Adams
2329 South Summit Circle Glen
Escondido, CA 92026
E-mail: cyberpoppa@juno.com

1

How Come It's Taking Me So Long to Get Better?

THAT SICK FEELING in the pit of my stomach, a mixture of hot anger and bewilderment, told me clearly that I had blown it again. As rapidly as my mind tried to justify my side of the argument, just as rapidly something else deep inside me shrieked "failure"! Another argument with my wife—harsh words, angry voices, accusations, and counteraccusations—arguing about the arguing —endless hurt, given and taken—and now the sullen silence with the swollen feeling of bursting rage.

Each time this recurring agony took place, our differences seemed more impossible to reconcile. A glimmer of hope in one area of the relationship would soon be shattered by deterioration in another.

As bad as all of this was, it wasn't the worst hurt, or the greatest confusion. That came because I was a minister of the gospel of Jesus Christ, and pastor of a wonderful band of Christian people, most of whom had come to believe in Jesus Christ because of me. I was the one who had told, and was telling, them that the living Jesus could heal their wounds and solve their problems. Moreover, I often had counseled them successfully in their marital difficulties without being able to solve my own.

I could cite verse after verse from the Bible, and my seminary training had given me gobs of information on the saving power of Jesus Christ, yet most of it seemed so ineffective in resolving my own difficulty. To make matters more bewildering, while a senior in seminary, I had been honored by Billy Graham with an invitation to join his Team for the first great New York Crusade in 1957. Because of that six-month experience I now had a reputation to live up to.

There were other areas of failure, though none

quite so threatening as the marriage difficulties. My own ego needs drove me compulsively in my work. Just serving God faithfully was not enough. I had to be leading the pack or, at the least, promising to lead the pack in time. Somewhere along the line, to make matters worse, I had equated church work as being the measure of my love for God. Successful church work equals big love for God. Keep so busy, give so much of your time, be available to everybody everywhere, accept every speaking opportunity, and do that to such an extent that just everybody will marvel at how dedicated you are. When they begin to express concerns for your health you know you're really impressing them. A friend once told me, "If a man is on fire for Christ, people will come if for no other reason than to watch him burn!" I needed the approval and attention of others so much that my compulsive activity was about to send me up in smoke. Educational deficiencies and my bizarre background (Navy fighter pilot, nightclub singer, and hotel manager, with a fling at banking and the auto business) drove me to feel I had to prove myself. Wife and child were usually given the short end of the stick in both time and quality of attention. In my blindness I usually interpreted any protest from them as an attack from the devil. So, the ego problem was feeding the marital difficulty.

As spiritual successes mounted in the church, personal failures were facing me with a searing question. In the light of everything I so strongly believed about Jesus Christ and had so dogmatically preached to my people, *Why, oh why, was it taking me so long to get better?* I would often get terrifying glimpses of where I was wrong. I would pray desperately about them, but progress was almost nonexistent so far as I could see.

At times I would begin to doubt that I had come into a saving relationship with Jesus Christ. The reason for this was obvious. All of my brief Christian life I had heard preacher after preacher shout, "If any man be in Christ he is a *new* creature, old things have passed away; behold, all things have become new!"[1] True, there had been a number of things that were new in my life and impossible to explain apart from Jesus Christ. There were also some old things that had passed away, but there were so many other old things in me that just wouldn't seem to die. Covered with a spiritual veneer, but still painfully known to me, their continued presence was a humiliation. Add to this the preaching and teaching which implies that every Christian should *always* exhibit the lofty, positive virtues of "love, joy, peace, longsuffering, gentleness, goodness, faith"[2] and you'll understand why I found myself near to despair.

The revolutionary change which had taken place in the Apostle Paul, plus the glowing testimonies of others about their contemporary experience left me confused over the sadly divided house in which I lived. I was divided as a man and as a husband. Neither problem responded to the crash programs I occasionally employed to alleviate the pressure. In both cases these efforts would often backfire and leave me deeper in despair. The more bravely I plunged on in my work, the greater my sense of hypocrisy.

At that time of my life and in my circle of friends there seemed to be just no one else who was plagued with my kind of problems. If they had them, they were as silent about them as I was. I lived in fear that someone would find out, yet I longed for some understanding, warm-blooded human to know how I hurt. In short, I had

become a prisoner of the very problem that lay
at the heart of my difficulties with my wife—no communication—not with her nor with anyone else—not
at a deep and honest feeling level. All of this
was hid from me at the time. (Only 20-20 hind-
sight has made it possible for me to see it, even now.)

In this struggle I often sought the counsel of
others by reading books, and by veiled and round-
about questioning of men that I admired. Never
admitting to the real specifics, I yet longed to
know more about what brought maturity in the Christian life because it was becoming obvious to me that
I didn't have it. (Oh! How hard it was for me
to face and admit this to myself!) There was general agreement on what brought maturity. Serious,
in-depth, daily study of the Bible; a living relationship to God in prayer; regular sharing of your faith
in Christ through witness; involvement in the local
church and other service to mankind as opportunities presented themselves. All of this I had
been doing for several years. Why were the results
not greater?

This introduced the subject of time; so, from
then on, my questions would also revolve around
the subject of how long it takes to become mature.
Bear in mind an important thing implicit in theological education. *It takes three years (usually)
to graduate from seminary.* At that point it is
assumed that you are mature enough to provide
spiritual leadership to a congregation of people,
many of whom have lived much longer than
you have, and have known God much longer than
you have. So, whether anyone actually came
out and said it, the implication was that three
intensive years of study and practical preparation
would make one mature enough to be a spiritual
leader. I had already had that, plus other learn-

ing opportunities which few others were privileged to experience. Yet, my problems were about to sink me.

To this question, of "How long does it take to mature spiritually?" I received almost no help at all from others. Answers ranged anywhere from a concept of conversion that presupposed maturity arriving overnight to an honest "I don't know." But even those who said they didn't know seemed to presume that it shouldn't take too long. Because none of us were really dealing with, or even admitting to, the specifics of our problems, we would retreat to Bible verse clichés and just keep on, hoping for the best.

But the pain of my own personal difficulties forced me to think, pray, and search for some insights that would relieve the building tension. But always the question was rising up inside me, *"How come it's taking me so long to get better?"*

2

The
Great
Invasion

INVASION! The word held a strange fascination for me. Not so much in the military sense as in the sense of what happened to a person at the time of his conversion. I had come to realize that when a person's faith led him to receive Jesus as Lord and Savior he was actually invaded by the same Spirit that had raised Jesus from the dead. Moreover, I really believed that was what had happened to me. There was ample evidence for it. I had changed. My questions were, "Why hadn't I changed more?", "How come it's taking so long?", and "Why do I still have such a problem with temptation and sin?" So you're invaded by the Spirit of Jesus. What happens then?

One day while thinking about this I went back in my mind to my Navy days in WW II. I took out pencil and paper, drew an imaginary island and relived the process of invading an enemy-held island. What I discovered changed my life.

In the Pacific during the early part of WW II the United States and her allies quickly lost their possessions island by island. An island-hopping technique was devised to regain the Pacific in order to protect Hawaii, Alaska, and California from an expected invasion by the Japanese.

Each enemy-held island was very carefully photographed and strategically considered to see whether or not it was important enough to be retaken. Some were bypassed. Others had to be recaptured if we were to regain the Pacific. These islands were photographed in great detail by aerial reconnaissance to locate the fortifications. Then would begin a very meticulous softening-up process against the enemy-held island. Headquarters would examine the photographs and begin an

aerial assault using rockets, bombs, and strafing to
knock out those areas of known strength. Several
areas of the island would be targets so that the exact
place of invasion would not be revealed. After
we in the aircraft had done everything we could,
the big ships with the more accurate long-range
guns would begin pinpoint shelling from off-shore.
The object of this process was sufficiently to weaken
the fortifications so when the troops landed
they would be able to secure beachheads.

ENEMY
HELD

Then the climactic moment would come
when the troop ships would deploy their
precious human cargo, the United States Marines.
And the Marines, having boarded their small land-
ing craft, would rendezvous and assault
the beach. By prearrangement they would come
onto the beach at a particular place and secure a
beachhead. This would be merely a fragment
of the island because they did not want to take
more than they had the troops to hold. They would
dig in, controlling that beachhead, and then very
confidently radio back to combat information center
saying, "The Marines have landed, and the situation
is well in hand." Now, anyone with an eyeball for
real estate can tell you that this was quite a
presumption on the part of the Marines, because they

held such a small beachhead on the island, and
the enemy, with all his genius, held all the rest.
No matter how badly he was battered, inevitably the surface of the enemy's defenses had hardly
been scratched when the men assaulted the
beach. (Anyone who was in Iwo Jima or Guadalcanal knows what that means.)

Now notice something about those Marines:
Never in the course of the war in the Pacific
were they pushed off an island. So, although it was
arrogant presumptuousness for them to radio back,
"Marines have landed, the situation is well in hand,"
the truth was that the situation *was* well in hand,
even though they only held a tiny piece of the
total island. As soon as the beachhead was secured
other craft would come and land heavier
equipment, such as tanks and artillery.

All this time the softening-up process continued
along the front, because the Marines never intended
to remain on the beach. They had not come for
a beach party. They had come to drive to the very
heart of the island eventually. When the situation
on the beachhead was secure and enough of the
heavy stuff was safely on the beach, they
would launch an offensive. Their intention was
to bite off another hunk of enemy-held territory,
secure it, then take another hunk, secure it, and
so on until the entire island was captured. About
the time they secured one piece there would be
another massive drive into another area to take
more of the island. This process would continue
until the entire island would become the possession
of the United States.

Why am I telling you this? Because I have just
drawn what is for me the most helpful picture of
Christian conversion and the Christian life that
I've seen. We are all islands of self in the hands

of the enemy. Conversion is like an invasion and the Christian life is like a war.

When we respond to the invitation of Jesus, "Behold, I stand at the door, and knock; if any man hear my voice, and open the door, I will come in to him, and will sup with him, and he with me,"[1] then the Holy Spirit of Christ invades us and establishes a beachhead in our lives. An enemy-held island now has inside it the invading force of our friendly God. He is beginning a conquest by love, not by tyranny, but we must always remember it is just a beginning.

There is a sincere but mistaken form of evangelism which gives the impression that the total conquest of the island is accomplished by the mere invasion. Both the Bible and human experience deny that this is the case, yet such notions persist, and when they are believed by the new Christian he is being set up for an agonizing experience in the not too distant future. The realities of life with the continual sin problem still staring him in the face will finally lead him to deny that reality, or he must assume there is something faulty with his conversion. Some begin to wonder if they are converted at all.

The important thing to see is that the initial reception of Jesus Christ brings an invasion of the human personality by God himself. John 1:12 says, "But as many as received him, to them gave he the power to become the sons of God. . . ." The beachhead God establishes is the beginning and that is instantaneous. The battle for the island called "you" is the long-range process of maturing.

In the Old Testament the Holy Spirit seems to have provided an external influence on a select few, while in the New Testament Jesus promises that the Holy Spirit will be internal, within the believer's body.[2] In the Old Testament even that external influence of the Holy Spirit might be withdrawn as in the cases of King Saul and Samson. In Psalm 51 David evidenced fear that the Holy Spirit might be taken from him. However, Jesus clearly states, "If you love me, obey me; and I will ask the Father and he will give you another Comforter, and *he will never leave you.*"[3]

So invasion is an apt word to describe what happens at the beginning of the Christian life—but the invasion only produces a beachhead.

But before the beachhead can be established there must come the softening-up process.

3

The Softening-up Process

IN EFFECT the Bible says we are each an enemy-held island. We are isolated and separated from God and others by a sea of sin, fear, and insecurity, and are dominated by self-centered urges that make us say, with the Apostle Paul, "My own behavior baffles me."[1] Separation from one another is the effect of our greater separation from God. The prophet Isaiah said, ". . . .but your iniquities have made a separation between you and your God, and your sins have hid his face from you so that he does not hear."[2] Because of this all of us tend to be like the man whose wife said, "My husband is like a mysterious island. I feel as though I've been circling in a little boat for twenty years, and never invited to land." It is only when we weary of this lonely island-like life that we begin to think of an alternative. It is the consequence of our sin that finally makes the pain of the isolation more than we can bear.

The softening-up process that precedes Christian conversion can take one of a hundred forms. Generally it involves a crisis of some sort brought on by the consequence of our own sin. There are occasions, however, where a tragedy that has no direct connection with our sin presents us with a situation we can't handle without God. I have seen people brought to the end of themselves in a multiplicity of ways. The "softening-up" process in my own case was hastened by marital disaster and a lack of vocational direction. I've seen others "softened up" by economic distress, alcoholism, sexual problems, career disappointments, political fear, drug addiction, absence of life purpose, shattering guilt, prison terms, ruptured relationships, consuming hate, and even disillusionment over success. Others have been "softened up" by the death of a loved one, while others have been touched by merely observing the transformation of another person being invaded by Jesus Christ. The different things that soften people up to the great invasion of God are as diverse as people and are as unique and original as God himself.

But whatever the crisis or situation that brings the process to a head, it is usually characterized by the individual's becoming aware of two things: that there is something too big for him to handle by himself; and that the God who directs this universe actually loves him and wants to take over his life and handle it for him. It is then that the admission that one is an enemy-held island will bring the invasion of the Holy Spirit. Jesus said, "Behold, I stand at the door and knock, and if anyone will hear my voice and open the door, I will come in to him. . . ."[3] For some of us a mere knock by the Lord was not enough. It was more like, "Behold, I stand at the door and bomb . . ." before we softened up to the point of seeing our need and God's sweet answer in Jesus. Nevertheless, better a Divine bomb than a continuation of our lives under the domination of a totalitarian devil.

So we saw our need and prayed that sweet prayer of new beginnings, "Come into my heart, Lord Jesus; make my heart your home!"

But then, what should one expect to have happen once he's prayed that prayer? So many testimonies would lead you to believe that all the old junk was gone overnight and that every little old thing became brand new just as quickly. It just didn't happen like that to me, as bravely as I tried outwardly to maintain that it did. The baby Christian wants so to please his new family that he's apt to play the game of "pretend" about his new life just to get the affirming response from his brothers and sisters. If he isn't told honestly what to expect, then his big mouth may lead him into the trap of spiritual hypocrisy. At the beginning it will all feel so good he may be quite a while realizing that his life doesn't really square with what his flapping lips insist.

Further confusion was added to my situation. It was marital discord which brought my wife to the point of suggesting that we read the New Testament looking for answers. It was during this time that Jesus became a living power in my life. He started the process of change in me, and many of our difficulties began to look far less threatening. Therefore, in my early efforts to share my new faith I would announce dramatically that Christ had saved our marriage. Now that was true, but you can imagine the confusion that followed when we continued to have difficulties. Because of where my public mouth was I tried to ignore those private problems in hopes they would just go away. Annette tried to help me face them but I found it nearly impossible to admit their seriousness, much less really deal with them. How could I admit to them when I had so often implied that my conversion had taken away those difficulties? Wouldn't this put Jesus Christ in a bad light? Wouldn't that be a lack of faith in his power to meet those problems? You can almost guess the next step, can't you? Sure! I put all the blame on my wife, and stupidly told her so. You can be quite sure that solved nothing. It only made matters worse, and understandably so.

What should receiving Jesus Christ do for me? Discernible growth makes things bearable. But, when things aren't getting any better, and are actu-

ally getting worse, hope begins to fade and doubt
begins to creep in. My good brother Lloyd Ogilvie
says, "Discouragement is the illegitimate child
of false expectations!"—and I was discouraged. My
expectations had been false because I had
not fully understood what had happened to me.

4

The Beachhead

JESUS CHRIST had captured a small beachhead in me in spite of the fact that I had "totally surrendered" my life to him. He had given me all of himself, but I could only give him as much of me as I knew and understood. There was so much of me that was hidden from my conscious awareness. He knew all about it but I didn't, and it would seem that Christ only goes where he is invited in a life. Because the data in that hidden part of my life was painful I had shoved it away from my own awareness. Moreover, I didn't want to face that part of me because of the pain it would bring. In a sense I wanted him to cure me of things that I was unwilling to admit were a problem. "Make me right, Lord, but don't ask me really to face what's wrong!" was often my attitude.

There were also things that I was *incapable* of facing at that time. The full and complete knowledge of those things all at once would have shattered me. But God in his mercy wanted me to face only so much as I could bear and deal with in a wholesome way.

God's Spirit had occupied a beachhead in my life. Where his forces were dug in there was love, joy, peace, longsuffering, gentleness, goodness, faith, meekness, temperance. But there was a great gob of me that wasn't occupied by anything other than my old sinful nature.

Usually, right after a conversion experience there is a period of pure, blissful peace *and I had it.* The joys of forgiveness, eternal life, and the love of Jesus swelled my heart to bursting. It was as though the forces of the old corrupt part of me had been shocked into quiet acceptance of the invasion of God.

Then there was that day when the peace and

quiet of my beatific beachhead began to shake with
the rumble of tanks, followed by the thump of
an artillery barrage as my own personal forces
of hell began a screaming counterattack on
God's beachhead. It was terrifying! Somehow,
somewhere, I had gained the impression that my
conversion to Jesus had laid all of those rotten
impulses to rest. Yet, here they were raging at
me with intensified fury.

As fearful as those things were, an ever greater
fear was that somehow the Lord had departed from
me. The guilt which accompanied the resur-
gence of evil impulses made me wonder if he had
just given up on me. I felt he would surely be justi-
fied in doing so. After all I was such a disappointment to *me,* what must I be to him? It was
a bewildering and frightening experience. At
times the misery was so intense that I was sure that
the only solution was to throw in the towel and give
up on the whole idea of being a Christian.
There were times when I tried to do just that. The
trouble was I had come to know the *truth* in
Jesus Christ and it no longer seemed that I had
the power to ditch him. *The fact* of him would not
go away, and somehow the light of that *fact* still
illuminated my way, even in the midst of self-
created darkness. Caught in such a dilemma I would
confess my sins to him, half-believing that it would
do no good and half-longing for that sweet
touch of his forgiveness. Of course, the
latter would be my experience, and in the joy of
another new beginning I would rush to promise him
all manner of perfection in the future to make up
for the past. That had built-in failure at the
heart of it because I was still not facing that unconquered part of my island that was ruled by my
old nature.

Just as I was penning that last sentence my phone rang and I heard the voice of a friend I had not heard from in eight years. My last contact with him had been during a Crusade in his home town. As a disc jockey he had interviewed me on the air and had listened while I had fielded telephoned questions from his fans, most of whom were teen-agers. However, neither my best efforts at witnessing to him, nor our growing friendship had brought him a step closer to any kind of commitment to Christ. But on the occasion of this call he brought to me the exciting news that he had come into a fantastic experience with Jesus Christ. "Man," he said, "I just gotta talk to you!"

When we got together he related a series of experiences with the living Christ that could only be described as startling and overwhelming. During this time he had also become an avid student of the Bible. He had experienced some truly amazing and ecstatic revelations of the living Christ. The problem was that these gigantic experiences had become less and less frequent, plus the fact that some of his old evil impulses were once again pushing at him for fulfillment. He was a living illustration of what I had just written. The invasion of God had been so spectacular that the forces of his old nature had been shocked into temporary quiescence. God had landed, the beachhead was secured. But when the dust settled he discovered that the enemy was still present in his island. Since he had not been led to expect this, serious questions about the validity of his conversion began to plague him, not to mention some sickening doubts about his sanity.

I shared with him in sketchy fashion some of the ideas I'm sharing with you. Relief came

from the realization that he fit the pattern of most
Christian people. But it was sobering for him
to realize that he was now in for a long war against
his entrenched old nature.

By now some of my readers have already begun
to think of some Christians they've known that
don't seem to fit this pattern of invasion which
produces only a small "beachhead." A word of
caution and a word of explanation are in order. First,
don't ever build your theology on human experience.
Our understanding of what God does in us has
to come from the Bible first. Conversion experience is valid only in so far as it is confirmed by
the Bible. Secondly, the only person we really know
about from the inside is ourselves. It has been my
experience to observe some new Christians
who gave the distinct impression that they were
riding a perpetual wave of spiritual victory. There
was no hint at all that they were experiencing any
of the grinding struggles I had. But when honest
sharing by fellow believers finally made them
feel safe enough to open up, the same pattern of
internal Christian warfare was revealed.

But both the Bible and Christian experience
would indicate one thing very clearly which helps
to understand the wide difference observed in
the impact of conversion on various people. That is
the simple fact that the initial size of God's beachhead varies from person to person.

5

How Big
Is Your
Beachhead?

HOW DO YOU FIGURE IT? Two people
are converted to Christ at the same time. Spiritually
speaking, one takes off like a scalded dog, and
the other is so slow in progress that a turtle looks
like a speed demon in comparison. I've seen
this happen both as an evangelist and as a pastor.
The temptation is to leap to a simplistic explanation which may run anywhere from doubting the
sincerity of number 2 convert to an outright
denial that the person is really a Christian. Either
way, number 2 is hurt, not helped, by such an
attitude of judgment, and number 1 may not be
able to handle the heady praise that will come his
way for his performance. Despair grips number 2
and pride creeps up on number 1.

All of us know that we ought to move toward
maturity, but few of us have ever really sat down
and figured out what it is like, or whether we
or others have arrived there. Too frequently the
standard for Christian maturity amounts to glib verbal expression of the gospel and observance of a
local code of don'ts. The first puts a premium on
how you can tell others the gospel and your own
personal experience. The second puts a premium on
things you're no longer doing that you used to do in
your pre-Christian days. The truth is that many of
us have done both of these things splendidly and
had lives totally devoid of love. According to
the Savior himself, love is the only standard by
which we may judge whether or not a believer
is truly a believer and on his way toward maturity.

One thing for certain, the babe in Christ is going
to have a hard time mustering even a vague reflection of the love of God in his life, and if someone
applies the standard of maturity to him that is found
in 1 Corinthians 13, it might well come near to

plunging him into a terrible pit of despair
over how far short he falls. I never will forget
how utterly miserable I felt after my first reading
of Henry Drummond's little classic, *The Greatest
Thing in the World.* There's nothing wrong with
a beachhead baby Christian reading a message like
Drummond's if there is somebody there to balance
it off with an understanding that it may take a
good long while for the baby to even begin to
be able to reflect what Drummond is talking about.
That's why it is so crucial that the babe in
Christ understand right from the outset a very
important thing.

That is, that his *position* in the eyes of God
is perfect from the moment he believes and receives
the Savior into his enemy-held island. His *position*
is based on who Jesus Christ is and what he has
done for him. It is only when we are secure in the
knowledge that our *position* is perfect in the sight
of God that we have the courage to either face up
to or admit that our *condition* is miserable. The work
of Jesus Christ was achieving that *position* for us
sinners, and the work of the Holy Spirit is to remedy
our lousy *condition*. Scripture spells this phenomenal fact out for us. It says, "For by that one
offering he made forever perfect in the sight of God
all those whom he is making holy."[1]

As a babe in Christ, I was forever plagued
with the distinct impression that my salvation was
going to be withdrawn for nonperformance. I was
quite sure that one day the Lord would simply have
to say to me, "I've been very patient with you,
Lane, but today you went too far and now it's all
over between us!" How much anguish I could
have been saved had I known of the security of
the believer right from the start. I needed to know
that my security was based on what Jesus is and

what he has done, rather than on what I am and what I have done, or for that matter, left undone.

I suppose that as a human being I have been so bound up in manipulative love that is always swapping things that I'm dumbfounded when confronted with a love like that which I can't shut off by my nonperformance. I can still relive the flash of sheer joy that my heart knew when I discovered that ". . . .He guarantees right up to the end that you will be counted free from all sin and guilt on that day when he returns. God will surely do this for you, for he always does just what he says, and he is the one who invited you into this wonderful friendship with his Son, even Christ our Lord."[2] It is only when my heart knows that kind of security that I can honestly face up to how small that beachhead may be that God has in my life. It is only when I rest in that kind of love and that kind of keeping power that I can honestly turn and face how much of the old nature there is in me. But then, that still doesn't answer why the size of individual beachheads varies to such a degree.

We Christians are greatly indebted to psychological research that has been talking for years about the difference between the conscious and the unconscious mind. Some of the early leaders even saw a connection between psychology and religion. Phillip Mairet notes that ". . . .with Jung the psychology of the unconscious merges into the realm of religion. . . ."[3] "The psychiatrist gradually came to the conclusion that, underlying the conflicts and resolutions of the conscious mind, there is an unconscious psyche, of unknown depth, perhaps unfathomably."[4] "Freud too, regarded the unconscious. . . .to be the repository of all the desires, ideas, and memories re-

jected and repressed by the conscious personality. . . ."[5] The conscious mind would then be that
area of our thinking capacity from which
we can have immediate recall of all current
and considerable past data. The unconscious
mind is filled with that data that is too puzzling
or painful or disgusting to allow into our conscious
awareness. Most would agree that neurotic behavior
develops when data in the unconscious mind dic-
tates activities in the conscious realm. Paul's already
quoted cry of exasperation about himself is a
classic illustration of this, "My own behavior
baffles me."[6] The interesting thing about that
comment of Paul's is that it was made after
Jesus Christ had far more than just a beachhead
in his life.

What I'm suggesting is that a person receives
Jesus Christ into the conscious part of his being.
The size of his beachhead then would be determined by the accuracy with which he can think
in reality about himself. I can only give as much
of myself as I know and understand to as much of
Jesus Christ as I know and understand. This
then would account for the varying impact of
conversion on different people. It would help to explain why at times a person chinning on the edge
of the gutter, who has faced the corruption of
his own heart, often makes far more dramatic
progress in the Christian life than, say, a person
raised in a superreligious atmosphere, who, in
his desire to give an outward religious performance,
has never really faced some of the deep and ugly
things that he has going on inside of him. His religion has demanded that he repress those things and
not even begin to face up to their presence in his
life. His denial of their reality just shoves them
into the basement where they haunt him as a

phantasm. When he faces these things with the security of a true believer and the sustaining power of the Holy Spirit, he can then admit them and by the power of God let Christ take over that part of his life as well.

Whenever newspapers or magazines diagram the progress of warfare they inevitably use arrows to indicate new points of aggressive penetration and advance by the opposing forces. Those arrows are an appropriate illustration of the piercing pain often associated with progress in the Christian life. Like the arrow indicating military penetration, the Bible says of itself, "For whatever God says to us is full of living power; it is sharper than the sharpest dagger, cutting swift and deep into our innermost thoughts and desires with all their parts, exposing us for what we really are."[7] In other words the move toward maturity involves the Word of God helping us to expose and face the garbage in our unconscious minds. All we need to do is to confess that that material revealed to us is true, and allow God to cleanse it and occupy the new territory which he has revealed to us. It isn't that God is ignorant of what lies in my unconscious mind. He isn't. "He knows about everyone, everywhere. Everything about us is bare and wide open to the all-seeing eyes of our living God; nothing can be hidden from him to whom we must explain all that we have done."[8] God has always known about all that reprehensible junk in the basement of our lives, the unconscious mind. With perfect timing, he is simply showing us new territory that he needs to occupy by the power of his Holy Spirit. He will never show us more than we can bear at one time.

I used to have growing pains as a kid, but they were nothing compared to the pain of spiritual

growth that has come to me as I've been forced to
face what I am essentially like in the depth of
my being. Again, how kind of God that he
has only showed me what I could bear and has patiently waited for me to continue to face up.

Notice something about that little diagram of
mine. The more you advance the front line of God's
invading force, the broader the front gets. This
means that the more we are occupied by God
the greater our view is of the corruption that yet re-
mains within us. Could this be why Paul
said in Romans 7:18, "I know I am rotten through
and through so far as my old sinful nature is concerned. . . ."?[9] That's the same chapter in
which he called himself a wretched man, yet
when one sees the maturity reflected in the entire
document of the book of Romans one can only assume that Paul had risen to a great level of maturity
to be able to pen such a document. Has it not
also been the testimony of outstanding Christians
over the years that the godlier a man was, the more
conscious he was of the corruption that yet remained
within him? Toward the end of his life Paul
still called himself, "the chief of sinners."[10]

God then takes only what we can give him
in the way of a beachhead. The problem is not "getting more of God," but letting God "get more
of us." The deeper problem is that there is a great
section of us with which we are not in touch,
in the unconscious mind. Until we get in touch
we can't give that part of ourselves to God.
Perhaps this is what Paul is talking about when he
says, "In my mind I want to be God's willing
servant but instead I find myself still enslaved to
sin. . . .There is something else deep within
me in my lower nature that is at war with my mind
and wins the fight and makes me a slave to the

sin that is still within me. So you see how it is; my new life tells me to do right but the old nature that is still inside me loves to sin."[11] We can take comfort in the fact that that which is hidden to us is revealed to God and that too is already under the blood of the cross of Jesus Christ. The knowledge of forgiveness in that area of our lives is applied when we are enabled by the penetration of the Word of God and the Holy Spirit to see what is wrong, admit it, and claim the sweet forgiveness that has already been made available.

Paul himself may have been on the verge of some really bad emotional problems when he met Jesus Christ on the road to Damascus. Consider his behavior; rigid, dogmatic, and violent, and all under a religious cloak. He assisted in the murder of Stephen, and I don't think we're demeaning the Apostle when we say he was in bad shape.

What happens in Christian conversion is this: the Spirit of God as the Lamp of the Lord progressively reveals the inner unconscious self. We get more and more of a revelation of what we're really like on the inside as the invading force of God begins to penetrate the unconscious. It's not a pretty picture that we find, but we are able to face it because of our *position*. We don't have to put on unnecessary masks because we are secure. We can, therefore, be honest and begin to cooperate with the invading force of God, finding out who we are, what we are, and what is really going on in our lives. It might be a very helpful exercise to go back and think seriously about your ability to think with accuracy about yourself at the time that you invited Jesus Christ to invade your life. You can't know where you are in the Christian pilgrimage until you know where you started. You can't get an accurate indication of your

progress unless you know that from which you
are progressing. Hold on to your secure *position* in
Jesus Christ or you can never bear to be honest
about your *condition*.

One of the things that I have discovered in the
quarter century that I have known Jesus Christ
is that God is much nicer than most of us have
imagined. It's so important to see him as a loving
and kindly and benevolent heavenly Father.
"As a father has compassion for his children,
so the Lord tenderly sympathizes with those who
revere Him. For He knows what we are made
of; He keeps in mind that we are dust."[12]

No matter how big your beachhead was at the time
of conversion, it still produced only a spiritual infant
with all the obvious needs of an infant. You
might even say that at our spiritual birth, regardless
of the size of the beachhead, all we ever really
amount to is "beachhead babies."

6

Beachhead Babies

CHRISTIANS have habitually demanded too much too soon from spiritual infants, commanding them to conform to patterns of maturity that it may have taken others years and years to attain. For many a "beachhead baby" this pressure is more than they can bear, so they flee from the source of the pressure.

When this happens many church people offer searing judgments on the baby Christian, the evangelist involved, and sometimes call in question the whole idea of evangelism.

If the church represents the spiritually mature, then it follows that it is the responsibility of the mature to relate themselves to the immature. The mature must accommodate themselves to the needs of the immature, and meet them *where* they are and see them for *what* they are.

These new Christians are spiritual infants with all the limitations of infancy. The parent takes care of the young child, particularly in infancy and in the years of dependence. The mature church must assume its role of loving parental responsibility in relation to the spiritual infant.

It is amazing, but true, that the average church will often expect more spiritual maturity from new believers than they will from most of their old-established members. When such maturity is not immediately forthcoming, then criticism is leveled. Certainly this request for a reversal of traditional thinking must be carefully supported by the Word of God.

According to John 3 there is such a thing as spiritual birth. This is not optional; it is necessary if one is to see the Kingdom of God. 1 Peter 2:2 indicates that there is a state of spiritual infancy from which we grow by the intake of the Word of God. Paul indicates in Colossians 1:28 that spiritual growth should culminate finally in spiritual maturity.

There will be little argument about spiritual birth or spiritual maturity, but almost no one seems to take seriously the intermediate stages demanded by the analogy of physical and spiritual life paralleling one another in a developmental process. While avoiding the absurdities inevitably involved in pressing the analogy too far, I do believe that for every stage of physical development there seems to be a corresponding stage of spiritual development.

Thus, in the process of time, utilizing God's appointed means of grace—the Word, prayer and sacraments—the inquirer moves through these various stages: from the nursery to the kindergarten, into the primary and junior stages of life, through the area of agonizing spiritual adolescence, into young adulthood, and finally into maturity.

However, I do not believe that we will be able to appreciate this process of growth until we really come to grips with what we mean by spiritual infancy.

The whole matter is greatly complicated by the chronological confusion that inevitably results when, say, a 40-year-old Ph.D. is at one and the same time a spiritual infant. We relapse into a humanistic process of reasoning which simply will not admit to the fact that all the limitations of infancy are his. We automatically expect and demand too much of him.

Only when we apply the limitations of physical infancy to this new spiritual creature will we see him in the proper light. Only then will we avoid the pitfall of expecting too much too soon.

(Certainly, knowledge acquired prior to conversion can be—and often is—rapidly assimilated in the new Christian framework with much benefit, but just as often it isn't and thus hampers sanctification.)

What is a newborn baby like? What does he do? What do you expect from him? A look at physical infancy will help us to know what to expect of the spiritual infant.

First, the newborn baby has a voracious appetite for a specific kind of food. The trouble is, he

can't feed himself. Someone who loves him must feed him. It is pointless to set the table with a banquet and then wonder why he doesn't show up. The food must be brought to him, and the nipple placed in his mouth. So also the babe in Christ. Someone who loves him must feed him with the milk of the Word until he learns to feed himself. The patient parent finally lives to see the babe learn to take care of nourishing himself.

Second, the newborn baby sleeps most of the time. As a new father I remember waking up in the middle of one night because of a strange quietness. No crying! I tiptoed over to the crib to admire my tiny offspring.

While standing there looking at the little form, in the half light, I was gripped with fear as I realized that I could not detect any evidence of breathing. For one moment of panic I contemplated the possibility that she was dead. For all the world she looked like it. Closer examination revealed that she was very much alive, and complaining over being so rudely awakened.

So it is with the babe in Christ. He will seem to be sound asleep so much of the time that you will even begin to wonder if there is any spiritual life there at all. Give him time; he'll wake up.

I recall the sound advice given me once by the late Dr. L. Nelson Bell, when I complained about a lack of evidence of spiritual life in some of my newer

church members. He said: "Lane, don't
dig up the seed to see if it is growing."

Be patient; the babe in Christ will spend less
and less time sleeping as he grows up. Accept the
fact of the work of grace *by faith,* and then rejoice
when God makes it possible to see the outward
evidence of spiritual life.

Third, the newborn baby makes a lot of noise
that doesn't make sense to anyone except the parents
who love him. This is so often true of the newborn
Christian. Tragically, many who are supposed
to be mature are quite put off with the utterances
of a baby-Christian, and react to them in unloving
ways that shock the soul of the infant believer
and inhibit his growth.

The super-orthodox are often the most guilty
of this, blasting the babe in Christ when he doesn't
parrot the party-line with just the right clichés and
accepted jargon.

Fourth, the newborn baby exercises almost
constantly when he is awake. But most of his exercising consists of meaningless, uncoordinated move-
ments of arms, head, and legs. In brief, he seems
to be going off in all directions at once, but he
never gets anywhere. But given time and patient
encouragement he will learn to get about so well
that he'll run a healthy parent ragged just trying
to keep up. This is so characteristic of the babe in
Christ that it hardly needs further application.

Fifth, the newborn baby is certain to dirty
his diaper with astounding regularity. Just as surely
the babe in Christ will, through spiritual failures,
do the same thing. Nothing tests the genuineness of
the spiritual parents' love more than this. Having
had an unrealistic expectation of the infant believer
they are mortified that his failure has caused
embarrassment to them.

I remember the times when we showed our
baby girl off for the first time to relatives or friends.
Eager to impress them with her outstanding
qualities, we would bathe and dress her to look
like the picture on a pablum box. On several occasions like this at the crucial moment of presentation she managed an odor so overwhelming that
even her parents found it hard to smile or be
enthusiastic. There was nothing wrong with the
timing of her infantile functions. We were
just expecting too much from a baby.

Spiritual pride is often so damaged by the failure
of a spiritual offspring that the infant is disowned
and responsibility for his actions is disavowed. The
Christian who would treat a spiritual babe in this way
had better hope that his Savior will not treat him
in the same fashion.

To his own spiritual infants Jesus said, "Now you
are clean through the Word which I have spoken
unto you."[1] We need to be ever present
with the cleansing Word for the stumbling babe.

We must remind the babe over and over again
that the initial love of Christ came to him in spite
of what he was, and that the continuing love of Christ
will come to him in spite of what he is, and never
because he has merited it with perfect conduct.
"If we say that we have no sin, we deceive
ourselves, and the truth is not in us. If we confess
our sins he is faithful and just to forgive us our sins,
and to cleanse us from all unrighteousness."[2]

We must warn the babe against expecting too
much of himself, while guarding him against com-
placency about the evil that is within him. He
must be reassured again and again that "if any man
sin, we have an advocate with the Father, Jesus
Christ the righteous."[3]

He must not only sense the forgiveness of God,

but also of God's servant. Often the babe will be able to sense the unconditional love of God through another Christian before he will be able to sense it directly from God.

Above all else the babe in Christ will respond to the unconditional love of Christ as it is expressed to him by another Christian, one who is willing to accept him as he is with all of his infancy showing, one who is willing to encourage even the slightest indication of progress, and who knowingly understands and accepts the inabilities, weaknesses, and failures.

I have avoided trying to spell out specific activities to accomplish the care and feeding of spiritual infants because I feel that a proper biblical *attitude* toward the babe in Christ must exist in order for the activities to have the desired effect in Christian growth.

The right activity with the wrong attitude can do more harm than good; the wrong activity with the right attitude may result in spiritual advance; but the optimum is the right activity with the right attitude.

In John 6:39 the Lord Jesus says, "And this is the Father's will which hath sent me, that of all which he hath given me I should lose nothing, but should raise it up again at the last day." Ultimately only Christ can keep what Christ has called and converted. But the instrument through which the Spirit of Christ may wish to work his keeping grace is you and me.

May our zeal for the will of God be such that we are willing to ditch old ideas and prejudices and see the initial grace of God in the babes for what it is, so that we may give ourselves utterly to the care and feeding of the infants that our Savior "should lose nothing."[4]

7

The Breakout

IN WORLD WAR II when the invading forces
secured their beachhead and were dug in,
they began receiving reinforcements in men and
equipment. During this build-up period, the
beachhead would be subjected to frequent
counterattacks which would have to be
repulsed. But even these attacks had their value.
It gave our forces the opportunity to feel out the
enemy and gauge both his strength and his ability.
It also was a time to discover his weak points, to
probe with patrols and plan for that moment
when a major assault against the enemy lines could
be launched.

Because these friendly forces were compressed
into a small area, it left them particularly vulner-
able. Therefore, the bigger the build-up the
more pressing the need to carry the attack to
the enemy and break out of the confining perimeters
of the beachhead. More maneuvering room was
needed, and that could only come by capturing
more real estate from the enemy.

ENEMY
HELD

So also the situation for the "beachhead
baby" Christian. In the last chapter we discussed
the patient "build-up" process which lands
the reinforcements of God in the beachhead area

of the new believer's life. There then comes
that crucial moment when the forces of God have to
break out of the original perimeters and capture
new territory in the life.

When a new believer has the input of the Word of
God, fellowship in prayer, and fellowship with
other Christian believers, it is inevitable that
the new wine of God's new life in him is going to
pressure a breakout. It may take time to build
up that pressure, but it will come. This is why
the Lord Jesus Christ likened the infusion
of his Holy Spirit into the believer's life to the
fermentation process that takes place in new wine.
He says, "And who would use old wineskins
to store new wine? For the old skins would burst
with the pressure, and the wine would be
spilled and the skins ruined. Only new wineskins
are used to store new wine. That way both are
preserved."[1] As new and flexible wineskins allowed
the expansion of the wine, so also the perimeters
of the believer's beachhead must be flexed and
ready to bulge out and encompass new territory as
the Spirit of God breaks out for growth.

Tragically, many Christians spend most of their
lives in a build-up process and never break out.
One can only marvel at how they can stand
the internal pressure that must be precipitated by
their attendance at church, listening to the
Word of God preached, plus what it must do to
them to see other Christians breaking out of their
perimeters and experiencing the new joy of
bringing new areas of their lives under the domination of the Holy Spirit. It is appalling that so
often the church has become the guardian of the
status quo, all the while preaching a gospel
of never ending change. What an irony this is!
But, perhaps it reflects the condition of members

lifted to a corporate level of stalemate.
Leighton Ford once said of the church, "It
would seem that the church only prepares to
move out after it has been run over from
behind!"[2] He was speaking of the church's
reluctance to take a forward stance and move out
in expressing itself on grinding social issues.
But perhaps the same illustration applies to the individual who has Christ in a beachhead in his
life, and only tends to move out when he, too, has
been run over from behind by shattering
circumstances that demand that he break out into
new patterns of growth.

I don't know of anything that makes me
cringe on the inside more than for somebody to clap
me on the shoulder, and say, "Good old Lane,
you never change!" It wouldn't be so bad if
comments like that were made about a person's
reliability, steadfastness, and reactions of
pure love, but in my case, it seems that each time
it has been said it was in response to some
reaction that I had evidenced that, indeed,
indicated a certain rigidity in me that made the
statement truer than I would like to admit.
For the Christian, change is the name of the game.
Not capricious or whimsical change, but purposeful,
steady change that is moving us toward
the specific goal that God has in mind for our
lives. This is what Paul was talking about when
he said, "So, whatever it takes, I will be
one who lives in the fresh newness of life of those
who are alive from the dead. I don't mean to
say I'm perfect. I haven't learned all I should even
yet, but I keep working toward that day
when I will finally be all that Christ saved me
for and wants me to be. No, dear brothers, I am
still not all I should be but I am bringing

all of my energies to bear on this one thing: forgetting
the past and looking forward to what lies ahead,
I strain to reach the end of the race and receive
the prize for which God is calling us up to
heaven because of what Christ Jesus did for us."[3]

And one thing we can all be certain of, that
is, that this pattern of God breaking out of the
perimeters that we have set for him is intended
by him to go on endlessly in our lives. At
least, that's the way it's been for me in the
quarter-century-plus that I've known Christ.
About the time I feel that I can really be
at ease in Zion I sense that God is readying
another build-up in order to launch another attack
on the enemy in me, and take new territory
that I have either had obscured from my
view deep in my unconscious mind, or have in
plain view and just out of pure stubbornness have
restrained God from getting into.

In World War II the genius of the Japanese
for concealment was amazing. They could dig into
caves and find places to hide that at times
seemed almost impervious to whatever we could
throw at them in order to root them out.

So also I believe that one of the tragic
misunderstandings of today's Christian world is how
basically corrupt our old evil nature really is.
I don't think that Jeremiah was kidding
when he said, "The heart is deceitful above
all things and utterly corrupt; who can know it?"[4]
One of the reasons why we have misunderstood
how long it takes to bring about maturity
is that we have *said* we believed statements like
the one from Jeremiah, but in actual fact we have
acted as though our corruption was of easy
and quick solution.

Jesus also echoed Jeremiah's estimate of the

condition of the human heart when he said,
"What comes out of the man defiles him; for from
within, out of a man's heart, wicked reasonings
proceed, unchastities, thefts, murders,
adulteries, covetings, wickedness, falsehood,
lewdness, an evil eye, blasphemy, pride,
thoughtlessness. All these wicked things come from
the inside and defile the person."[5] If we

really faced the depth of corruption that exists in
that unconquered part of our islands and admitted
the same, I don't think that we would be quite
so surprised over the bickerings and divisions,
criticisms and downright hostilities that are
often evident between sincerely redeemed people
inside the church. Perhaps my problem is
the problem that everyone else has: I'm perfectly
delighted to recognize all of this corruption in
everyone else but hard put to it to face it
within myself. It is only when I do face this condition in me and welcome the build-up of God's
forces that I am prepared to cooperate and
even hasten the breakouts in my life that God
wants to accomplish. Most of us want God
to do more about the evil in the world, but few of
us really want God to start working on the
world's evil by working on the evil in us.

So, regardless of where we are in our Christian
life, whether beachhead babies, or people
whose island is half occupied by the forces of God,
we can rest assured that God wants to break
out of the perimeters we have established for
him. As in war, there will be death and
bloodshed to accomplish this objective. I've come
to believe that this is what Paul meant
when he said, "I die daily." The advance of the
life of God is dependent upon the death of
another part of self. Why I resist God's

breakouts to such an extent is a puzzle to me.
Especially when I remember that in spite
of the pain of dying to self, there is such great
joy and comfort in having a new area of
my life occupied by the Spirit who brings love and
joy and peace to that area.

A comedian friend of mine used to tell
the story of a man who took Carters Little Liver
Pills all his life. He said that when that
fellow died, they had to take a big stick and beat
his liver to death. I really identify with that
classic illustration of the enemy-held part of me. That
part of me is worse than a cat for having nine
lives. Instead of taking a big stick to beat it
to death, I take the sword of the Spirit,
which is the Word of God, and give it a good
going over every day.

"Onward Christian Soldiers" would be a good
hymn to sing at the beginning of every day, but only
if we realized that the war that we're marching to
is far more internal than it is external.

8

Whose Side Are You On?

I HAVE NO IDEA where this story started. It's too good an illustration not to use simply because you don't know the source. An old preacher was once asked what it felt like on the inside to be a Christian. He silently mused on the subject for a bit and then said, "Well, it's sort of like I've got two dogs inside of me. One is a good dog and the other is a bad dog, and they's always fightin'!"

His questioner, wanting more information, said, "Which dog is winning the fight?"

"Whichever one Ah says, 'sic 'em' to!"

Isn't that description a beaut? A punch line on that story that is equally profound—when asked which dog is winning, the answer is, "Whichever one Ah feeds!" Either way the story is told it presents us with a very basic question that has to be answered not only once, but almost on a daily basis.

The question is, *Whose side are you on* in this private war that you've got going on inside yourself? You might say, well, doesn't a person decide when he invites Jesus Christ to invade his own personal island that he is on God's side, and that's settled? Well, theoretically, I suppose, it is settled, but in actual practice I find that I have to re-settle that issue day after day. For instance, every day I have to decide whether I'm going to feed the new nature on the Word of God and prayer and fellowship with likeminded believers, or whether I'm going to do those things that will actually co-operate with the worse side of me. I find I'm great for theory in broad sweeping generalizations, but often hard put to it to work that theory out in practical daily experience in which I'm actually obedient to the commands of God.

One such command would be Jesus' statement, "But seek ye *first* the Kingdom of God and his righteousness, and all these things shall be added unto you."[1] Just today, for instance, after an exhausting schedule last night, I couldn't manage to struggle out of bed at the hour my clock went off, and it set everything running late so that my time of devotions got squeezed out. Like a jerk I sacrificed the best for something that was really quite good. I wanted to get on with writing this book, but didn't really give enough time to feeding the new nature and saying "sic 'em" to the Holy Spirit at work in my island.

Yes, I'm still having this struggle on a daily basis, even after knowing Christ over a quarter of a century. I would gather that Paul wrote the book of Galatians about the time when he had known Christ somewhere between twenty and thirty years, so I'll simply cite what he said. "I advise you to obey only the Holy Spirit's instructions. He will tell you where to go and what to do, and then you won't always be doing the wrong things your evil nature wants you to. For we naturally love to do evil things that are just the opposite from the things that the Holy Spirit tells us to do; and the good things we want to do when the Spirit has his way with us are just the opposite of our natural desires. These two forces within us are constantly fighting each other to win control over us and our wishes are never free from their pressures."[2] It would seem from this that Paul was making daily decisions concerning whether or not to obey the Holy Spirit's instructions, or whether to follow his natural (and I might add, normal) inclinations to pursue what his old enemy-held nature wanted him to do.

As a matter of fact, he goes on to indicate what happens when you don't obey the Holy Spirit's instructions. He says, "But when you follow your own wrong inclinations your lives will produce these evil results: impure thoughts, eagerness for lustful pleasure, idolatry, spiritism (that is, encouraging the activity of demons), hatred and fighting, jealousy and anger, constant effort to get the best for yourself, complaints and criticisms, the feeling that everyone else is wrong except those in your own little group—and there

will be wrong doctrine, envy, murder, drunkenness, wild parties, and all that sort of thing. Let me tell you again as I have before, that anyone living that sort of life will not inherit the Kingdom of God."[3] It might be well to ask ourselves a question, "How did Paul know that following your own natural, evil inclinations would produce that kind of result?" The answer probably is that some of that he observed in others, but a great deal of it he observed in himself. So, there is really a basic decision that we need to come to: *Whose side are you on?* Paul put it this way, "Don't you realize that you can choose your own master? You can choose sin (with death) or else obedience (with acquittal). The one to whom you offer yourself—he will take you and be your master and you will be his slave."[4]

There is a sense in which we do make an initial decision to make Jesus Christ and his Spirit our Master by declaring that we intend to obey him. But there is also a sense in which if we are going to make periodic breakouts and advances in this internal war, that we are going to have to cooperate with God by participating and allowing him to have a daily buildup within us to prepare for that next breakout in which he takes new territory. Since almost no one has really faced how long it takes to move from being a beachhead baby to being a well occupied

island or, in other words, to go from spiritual
infancy to spiritual maturity, well-meaning but misguided Christians have consistently implied that
one can have instant maturity. I'm well aware of
the fact that if pressed on such a contention,
people would deny that that's really what
they're saying. But whether explicitly or implicitly,
that is actually what is often heard by the baby
Christian. We live in a day when we can get
instant coffee, instant iced tea, and even
instant grits (thrown in for the benefit of any
Southern readers). But I deny categorically the
possibility of instant spiritual maturity. The
danger is that people are offering what look like
beautiful shortcuts to becoming a mature believer.

The first shortcut is the trap of legalism.
Legalism is the notion that Christian maturity is
demonstrated by certain negative behaviors.
If you perform these negative behaviors by not
doing this, or not drinking that, or by staying
away from this place, or not engaging in that habit,
then the idea is, you indicate that you have moved to
spiritual maturity. Some churches even take
these rules that are basically manmade and
put them on signs prominently displayed in the
church house. Christian institutions of higher
learning oftentimes require students to sign
a pledge concerning these negative behaviors.
Whereas they do not come right out and indicate
that performance of the pledge automatically
makes you mature, it is at least there by implication.

Paul very directly spikes the incapacity
of legalism to accomplish maturity when he
says, "So don't let anyone criticize you for what you
eat or drink, or for not celebrating Jewish
holidays and feasts or new moon ceremonies or
sabbaths. For these were only temporary rules

that ended when Christ came. They were
only shadows of the real thing—of Christ himself. . . .
Since you died, as it were, with Christ and this
has set you free from following the world's
ideas of how to be saved—by doing good and
obeying various rules—why do you keep right on
following them anyway, still bound by such
rules as not eating, tasting, or even touching certain

foods? Such rules are mere human teachings, for
food was made to be eaten and used up. These
rules may seem good, for rules of this kind
require strong devotion and are humiliating and hard
on the body, but they have no effect when it comes
to conquering a person's evil thoughts and desires.
They only make him proud."[5]

I was speaking at a conference one day on this
subject, and after I sat down my friend Fred Smith
got up and offered three penetrating reasons why
legalism would never do for bringing maturity. His
three reasons were: (1) a legalistic list of behaviors lets you know when you "arrive" and, therefore, produces pride. (2) Keeping a list of rules
lets you know who you are better than, and that
produces pride. (3) With the devious nature of the
human mind any list of legal rules was designed
to be "got around."

Just find a legalistic group of Christians and
I'll show you a bunch of people who are
usually looking down their noses at others who
are not following the rules that they have set up. The
funny thing about it is that this concept of maturity
is very geographical. All you have to do is
travel a few hundred miles and the list
of rules changes. If you go to a different country,
you oftentimes find radical differences in what
fits the list. Jesus said it, and it still stands,
"By this shall all men know that you are my

disciples in that you have love one to another."[6]

One of the grave dangers of a purely legalistic approach to the Christian life is that it tends to produce a vacuum in the life. When Christian maturity is equated with the removal of bad habits, instead of their replacement by the invading power of the Holy Spirit, the emptying process may in itself cave in a new Christian. The illustration of an empty glass is pertinent to this point. How do you get all of the air out of an empty glass? Anyone who knows anything about physics knows that there is no such thing as a perfect vacuum, and if you should try to get all the air out of a glass, the atmospheric pressure would make it collapse. So also, the life from which bad behavior habits are removed without an adequate replacement. One can get all the air out of a glass simply by filling it with water. The air is forced out of the glass by what's coming into it. Ideally, this is the way unbiblical behavior should be forced out of a life—but merely to make of the Christian life the negating of unbiblical behavior will produce a vacuum. The pressure of the world will often cave a young Christian in if he has been taught this way of instant maturity.

Another legalistic trap that has to be carefully spiked is the notion that a Christian education produces maturity. The theory seems to be that if you just cram enough Bible facts and theology into a person's skull, it is automatically going to produce maturity. It has surely been my observation that the mere acquisition of information does not automatically produce spiritual maturity. As a matter of fact, it can produce frustration of the most gigantic sort. The reason is not hard to find.

Oftentimes, when you have jammed tremendous information about the requirements of the Christian life into a person's head, it produces frustration because he can think so far beyond where he can perform. His theory is so much better than his practice that he is overwhelmed with a gigantic sense of guilt over his own hypocrisy. Simply knowing something does not produce in the knower the automatic capacity for doing. Consequently, when a person acquires a gigantic amount of information in a hurry, he may be almost totally immobilized over his inability to implement the demands of that information in his own life. Certainly, I'm not against education. I think it is a crucial aspect of Christian nurture. But cram courses are often inflicted on people readying themselves for church related vocations. This puts them next to despair because their lips can so far outdistance their lives. If this were my isolated experience, I would be ready to accuse myself of projecting my needs to others. But in my contact with clergy all over the English-speaking world I have come to realize that many of them have experienced and are experiencing precisely this frustration. Tragically, never having been warned about such a possibility, and having no one else talk openly about it, they falsely assume that they, and they only, have this problem. Jesus said, "If you know these things, happy are you if you do them."[7] It stands to reason then, if our knowing outruns our doing that we are going to be grossly unhappy.

One night Annette and I were eating in a restaurant, and just as we were finishing our meal, two young men and a young lady came over to our table and introduced themselves. Their address and manner indicated that

they were people who had found Jesus Christ
right out of this modern street scene. The
one was carrying a Bible big enough to serve any
church as a pulpit Bible. They had heard me
speak somewhere and came over to have
a bit of fellowship. None of the three had been
Christians for very long, but all were quite
eager in their new life in Jesus Christ. Later, as we
were driving home, Annette said to me, "Those
kids are quite amazing, aren't they? They know so
little, but they are doing so much of what
they know, whereas we know so much and do so
little of the total that we know." Perhaps the
very reason for the radiance and happiness of those
kids was that they were proceeding at a rate of
doing that matched the acquisition of what
they were learning.

I'm aware of the fact that you can't do
something until you know it, and that therefore the
acquisition of knowledge has to be accomplished
prior to implementing that knowledge. What
I am suggesting is that we too frequently
oversell the effectiveness of acquiring a great deal of
knowledge in a hurry. I believe that our
education process should blend the sharing of
knowledge with the capacity to implement that
knowledge in the life.

Could this possibly be why the writer of
Ecclesiastes said, "I applied my heart to know
wisdom and knowledge, madness and folly. I
discovered that this, too, is chasing after
wind. *For in more wisdom is more vexation, and
increasing one's knowledge increases one's distress.*"[8]
Our beloved friend Pat Hunter once said,
"King Solomon wrote two thousand proverbs and
when the chips were down he couldn't find
the capacity to obey them." In other words, his

knowledge gave him the ability to see and
even to teach so much better than he could do.

It's interesting to note that only Jesus of
Nazareth, among all of the religious figures
of the world, was able to live up to the standard of
behavior which he taught. Perhaps one of the
things we should carefully rethink is the
pace we set in imparting knowledge to a new

Christian. Jesus alone could do what he knew.
Could it be then, that cramming people too full of
information may actually end up being a distress
if they have no ability to implement anything
more than a fraction of this knowledge?

The other trap that has so often been sincerely
offered to the new Christian, and to the
old, as a shortcut to maturity has been the "special
experience." This might range from a blurb in a
brochure announcing a special conference—
"Come to this conference and get it all together!"—to
those Christian groups that are advertising the
idea that a special experience of the Holy Spirit
is going to really get you over the hump and
on the right side of maturity. I do not deny in any
way the possibility of one being "filled with
the Spirit." What I do deny—and I think the
Bible supports me—is the idea that anyone is
ever totally filled with the Spirit to the extent that he
obliterates that enemy-held part of him which is
in his unconscious mind. To indicate such
implies a perfectionism that is not reflected in any
Christian life I have ever seen. It surely is not
reflected in mine, although I have "totally
surrendered" and "asked for the filling of the Spirit"
on innumerable occasions. What usually had
happened on such occasions was that the Holy
Spirit had revealed a new area of my life that needed
to come under his dominance. My new total

surrender was the giving up of territory that I did
not know about until the Holy Spirit revealed it
to me. I surely do not despise, disparage, nor
in any way invalidate these experiences. I'm
suggesting that what they add up to in the long
run is simply the capture of more territory by
the Holy Spirit. In other words, the Holy Spirit has
broken out of the perimeters that we had established for him, and in this new experience he has taken
new territory.

I was asked once to bring a message to
the entire Christian education department of
one of the most dynamic Pentecostal churches I
have ever seen. They fully believed in the filling
of the Holy Spirit, and as far as I know,
they still do. However, when I drew the diagram
of the enemy-held island and the invasion, the
establishing of the beachhead and the concept
of breakouts, there was general acknowledgement
that this was precisely that which had been
their experience. I spoke directly to the
issue of being filled with the Holy Spirit and
the experience of "speaking in tongues." I asked this
question, "Isn't it true, that after you had
spoken in tongues, experienced the fullness of
the Holy Spirit, and had lived with this for a
period of time, you discovered that the
actual impact in your life had been somewhat
oversold before you had experienced it? Isn't
it true that what actually happened was that God got a
new section of your enemy-held island, but he
did not in any way take the whole thing at
the time?"

The responding chorus of "Amen!" let me
know that I had struck a deep responsive chord in
their understanding of the nature of what had
happened to them in this "special experience."

Paul speaks directly to this situation of the special experience in the same chapter in which he spiked the inefficiency of legalism. He says, "Don't let anyone declare you lost when you refuse to worship angels, as they say you must. They have seen a vision, they say, and *know you should.* These proud men have a very clever imagination. But they are not connected to Christ, the head to which all of us who are his body are joined; for we are joined together by his strong sinews and we grow only as we get our nourishment and strength from him."[9]

What I hear Paul saying here is that all of us tend to want everyone else to have the same kind of experience that we have had. In this regard we always tend to want everybody to be converted in the same way we have been, or else we tend to look with some skepticism on the reality of their conversion. It's interesting that he also teaches in this passage that both the legalism and the "special experience" people are made proud by this dogmatic stance which they take and apply to everyone else. Friend, there is no such thing as instant maturity. I know of no shortcuts whatsoever in the realm of spiritual growth. In the next chapter we'll talk about how long it takes to arrive at a reasonable level of maturity. But for now I want to address myself to one more deep problem that comes out of this business of demanding that someone else have the same kind of "special experience" that we have had.

Any experience of the grace of God necessarily thrusts us into the realm of feelings. I know of nothing more difficult to describe than "a feeling." Recently I led a class of new members in a prayer of commitment wherein they received

Jesus Christ as Savior and Lord and asked to be
filled with the Holy Spirit. The following
week a lady posed the question that she had really
expected that more would happen as a
consequence of receiving the Holy Spirit. When
I pressed her for what she meant, it got down to the
fact that she had thought that there would
be some sort of overwhelming feeling attendant
to that act of faith. When I asked her to describe the
kind of feeling she anticipated, she hesitated,
and then said, "Well, I expected to have
some sort of an overwhelming good feeling."
I then asked her, "What does a good feeling feel like?"
Then she floundered and simply responded, "Well,
it feels good!" I suggested this to her, "Don't
you suppose that a member of the Mafia feels
good when he has just killed his worst enemy?"
She agreed that he probably would, and then I
asked her to define the difference between his
feeling good and the kind of "feeling good"
that she thought ought to attend the act of faith
that I had led her in. This helped her see how
treacherous it was when we tried to define feelings.

If we must have a "proper religious feeling,"
then how would we know if we'd had the
right kind of feeling when we admit that feelings
vary so and that definition is so impossible to
accomplish. I am not saying that the reception of
Jesus Christ and the filling of the Holy Spirit
does not have as a by-product the possibility
of feelings. What I am saying is that the danger of
the special experience is the tendency to put
one's faith in one's feeling rather than in the never-
changing Word of Christ. In my own experience
I lived the life of a spiritual yo-yo in the
early stages until I learned that faith is to believe
what God had said in spite of what I might feel.

It was then that my spiritual life began to level out. A sinus headache didn't make me feel that God had abandoned me, because the Word of God still said the same thing—that he loved me, and that he would never leave me nor forsake me. Paul says, "For we walk by faith, not by sight."[10] When you remember that sight is a sense perception, I do not believe it is straining the verse at all to paraphrase it, "For we walk by faith and not by feeling." I thank God when good feelings attend me, but I believe God when I am devoid of feelings that might confirm the reality of the truth of Jesus Christ.

One day in 1969 I was walking down a New York street with my friend Jerome Hines, of the Metropolitan Opera company. "Jerry, how are you and the Lord getting on?" I asked him.

He smiled down at me from the three- or four-inch advantage of his six-foot-six height, and replied gently, "Lane, the longer I live, the more I think of Jesus and the less I think of me."

What an excellent antidote to the toxic effect of concentrating on ourselves and our feelings!

Perhaps the greatest treachery found in an undue reliance on feelings is revealed when you look ahead toward the end of life. As one grows older the strong tendency of the majority of us is to feel worse than we did when we were young, vibrant, and full of the vitality of youth. And, in the process of time, we feel so bad one day that we die. This means that the person who is relying on his feelings to confirm his belief would discover that at the time he needed that reassurance the most, it would be the farthest from him.

I think of the story told me recently by a friend concerning her grandmother. The dear old saint had lived to be ninety-nine years old, had suffered a

great deal, and was quite infirm and losing
strength rapidly. Toward the end she exclaimed,
"The music is beautiful! Please turn it up!" Then she
called out to a daughter who had died when she
was only fifteen years old. Then to her mother
and dad. Just as suddenly she seemed to be back in
the full reality of this life, and with a smile on her
face said, "Of course, you couldn't turn up
the music, because you couldn't hear it!" I'm quite
certain that the dear old lady felt pretty
awful at the moment that she had this gigantic
revelation of what lay just beyond the veil of this life.
As a matter of fact, in just a few moments after
that she had left this life and was in the next.
Her faith had sustained her in her hour of greatest
need, and the presence and power of Jesus Christ
had brought forth a magnificent reassuring experience
in spite of the fact that physically she felt wretched.

Add to this the glowing testimonies of so many
hundreds and thousands of people who have
suffered much in this life in a physical way and yet
have had gigantic expressions of faith in Jesus
Christ which was devoid of any physical feelings.

These are illustrations of what it is to walk by
faith. So, beware of the "feeling trap" that is
part and parcel of that oversold promise of a
"special experience" that is somehow going to get you
home free to the area of maturity. How sincerely
the promise is offered, yet the "special experience"
only gains more new (and sometimes very important) territory for the Holy Spirit.

Let me offer one other word about the
importance of putting feelings in their proper place.
We live in a time in history when people have
been tyrannized by their own feelings. Particularly is
this so in the younger generations. There
is a strong tendency to do only that which one

"feels" like doing. There is no question that how one "feels" is important, but the real issue is what has caused one to feel the way he does feel.

Some years ago in a meeting convened by Dr. Norman Vincent Peale, there was a group of us who had been brought together for the purpose of getting to know and trust each other. No organization was planned, nor ever came out of that meeting. Basically, we were there to share what we had learned about evangelism, and some of the outstanding figures in that field were present. In the course of the meeting a well-known practicing psychologist told of a trauma that he had been going through in his own life because, he said, "I have discovered that feelings follow behavior instead of the other way around. Since all of the education in my profession has insisted that behavior is a result of one's feelings, it has been a trauma to unlearn the one and embrace the other." I asked him to expand on this startling announcement, suggesting that if what he said was right, it would revolutionize what was being taught in this realm. Seminaries and colleges would have to alter their psychological doctrine to embrace such a radical notion. By the time he had offered his rationale to support this contention, I was fully convinced.

Out of my own life it makes sense. Misbehavior has always produced a feeling of guilt in me. Guilt makes me feel lousy. How about you? Whenever I resist the temptation to do wrong, and my behaviors are right according to God's Word, I inevitably feel good about it.

How often though in my own life I have been so tyrannized by my feelings that I was reduced to immobility. One of my favorite indoor sports

has always been to feel sorry for myself.
Yet, I discovered an easy way out of the deep
depression that afflicts me when I feel sorry for
myself. Jesus said, "Whatsoever that you would
that men should do to you, do you even
also unto them."[11] When I'm tyrannized by my
feelings and become immobilized by my self-pity, I can
sit down and make a list a yard long of good
things that I wish other people would do
for me. All I have to do is take number one on
my list and do it for someone else, and the
dark clouds of depression begin to dissipate
in the warm sunshine of one simple act of
obedience. Let me go as far as number two or three
on the list and I am almost hysterical with joy.
Feelings do follow behavior when the behavior is designed to make the life obedient to the
loving word of Jesus Christ. "If you know
these things, happy are you if you *do* them."[12]
When you know what he wants and you do it,
you discover that the good doctor was right
—feelings do follow behavior.

Then how do we maintain a regular, steady
advance on that enemy-held part of our island? By
realizing that we are in for a long pull, and that
it's going to be a battle against that lesser
self all the way. We've got to decide whose side
we're on and cheer the Holy Spirit on as he seeks to
search out new territory to reveal to us in order
that we can surrender it to him. We've got to feed
God's side of this struggle with the only food
that God has ever offered—his Word. It was Jesus who
said, "Man shall not live by bread alone, but by
every word that proceeds out of the mouth of
God."[13] We must build up the invading force of
God with the kind of ammunition that he can
use in this struggle. It's going to be a long war.

9

It's a Long, Long War

IT IS HARD TO IMAGINE anything more
discouraging to a new Christian than to
discover that he is still afflicted with patterns of
temptation and sin that he had come to Christ in order
to get rid of. It's one thing to make an occasional
blunder, but it's quite another thing to fail
again and again in the same pattern of
behavior. This is the kind of failure that I knew
and described in chapter 1. It can manifest
itself at the point of anyone's weakness. Doubts
begin to creep in about either the reality of one's
conversion or the power of Jesus Christ to deliver on
what he has promised.

The reason for this is that most of us have
been oversold, or misunderstood what was
going to happen to us when we receive Christ into
our lives. Plugging along in the Christian life,
we keep hoping and praying that something will
come along and a magic, overnight, total
transformation is going to take place. It was while
I was in seminary, having known Christ for
about four years, that I began to ask people this
burning question in my soul. How come it's
taking me so long to get better? I just never
could get a satisfactory answer that seemed to
help me with my understanding. Then one day years
later, in my Bible reading I ran across two verses
in 1 Timothy. Here Paul says, "Reliable
is the message and deserving of wholehearted
acceptance that Christ Jesus came into
the world to save sinners, of whom I am foremost.
But I found mercy, so that to me, foremost, Jesus
Christ might display his *unlimited patience,*
to be an *example* to *all* who shall put their trust in
Him for life eternal."[1]

I have italicized the words that leaped

out from the pages of the Bible and gripped
me with a life-transforming understanding.
Here in verse 15 Paul is announcing that Jesus
Christ came into the world to save sinners.
His use of the word *save* indicates the security of the
position that he knew he occupied because of the
finished work of Christ. But the phrase
of whom I am foremost indicates that
he still saw that his condition needed gigantic
continuing work by the Holy Spirit.

It was verse 16 that really got to me. Paul was
stating that his life was an example, or as other
translations put it, a pattern. He was offering
his life as that example to be looked to in
order to gain understanding about how God deals
with the worst of us, as well as the best of us.
By the use of the word *all* he indicates that his life
example was to apply to every believer in
the future, not just some. I hasten to add that it
means then that his life was an example
for the simplest believer, as well as the most profound
theological professor, the weakest saint, as well
as the strongest. It means everybody, and I'm
grateful for that, because that includes me.
But the greatest relief came to me when I saw that
Paul was stating that his life was an example
of the *unlimited patience of God.* It was when I read
those exciting words that I realized that patience
demands the employment of time. As my
dear professor Dr. Manford George Gutzke used
to say, "To be longsuffering (patient) one
has to be long-bothered!" I had been agonizing
over why my Christian development was so
perilously slow, and now here was the invitation of
God to examine the life of Paul to see how
long it took him to get to a point of maturity.

With great excitement I flipped my Bible to the two

places I knew to be either biographical or autobiographical concerning Paul's life. I turned to Acts, chapter 9, which relates the conversion experience of Paul, and then I turned to Galatians, chapter 1, which was an autobiographical testimony that I remembered employed some indication of how much time had passed by in his life.

I urge you to read all of Acts 9 through Acts 13:3. The passage in Galatians is 1:13 through 2:2. You can condense what you are going to find by comparing and collating these two sections about the passage of time. What we are looking for is the discovery of how long it took Paul to get to a point of maturity where he could bear big responsibility. The chapters in Acts go from his conversion to his ordination for missionary service. As you know, Paul was a terrible persecutor of Christians. He did it for God's sake, he thought. Not content with making havoc of the Church in Jerusalem and Judea, he got the authority to go to Damascus where some Christians had fled, in order to bring them back to Jerusalem and throw them in jail. The Bible clearly states that the Apostle Paul's zeal in persecuting Christians was so severe that he helped to incite the mob that stoned Stephen to death, holding their coats while others obviously actually did the deadly deed. It's hard to imagine anybody more anti-Christian than Saul of Tarsus.

On the way to Damascus he sees a great light, he hears a voice which he discovers is the voice of Jesus. Blinded by what he has seen and stunned by what he has experienced, he is led by the hand into the city of Damascus. A frightened layman, Ananias, is sent by God to lay his hands upon Paul and pray for him that he

might receive both the Holy Spirit and his
sight. Ananias' prayer is answered, and Paul
is fully converted to Jesus Christ. In his Galatians
reporting of the same event that Dr. Luke reports
about in Acts, he says, "I did not speedily com-
municate with flesh and blood, neither did I go
up to Jerusalem to those who were apostles
before I was, but I went away into Arabia and
came back to Damascus."[2] Immediately in verse 18,
"Then after three years I went up to Jerusalem
to get acquainted with Cephas [Peter] and
stayed in his company for fifteen days; but I
saw no other apostle except James, the
brother of the Lord. And what I am writing to
you, observe in the presence of God that I am not
falsifying."[3] Exactly what point in time during this
three-year period Paul went into the Jewish
synagogue and preached is not clear, but Acts
simply says, "After considerable time [this phrase
undoubtedly includes the three years that
Paul is talking about in Galatians 1] the Jews
conspired to destroy him, but Saul got wind of their
plot. Day and night they watched the gates to kill
him; but his disciples took hold of him and by
night let him down over the wall in a basket."[4]
The main thing to see is that either way you look at
the sequence of events in Damascus and Arabia,
it was three years before Paul went up to
Jerusalem for the first time. The passage in
Galatians confirms this. But after the Arabian
and Damascus three-year period he went up to
Jerusalem. Now, get a load of this! The relationship
between Damascus and Jerusalem was good in
those days. Trade routes were open, and Christians were on those trade routes. Jerusalem
undoubtedly had heard about Saul of
Tarsus, and what had happened to him on the

way to Damascus. In the three-year span there
must have been a reasonable amount of
communication that had arrived in Jerusalem to let
them know something of the significant events
surrounding Saul of Tarsus. *Yet,* when he
arrived in Jerusalem after that three-year time of
meditation in the desert and communication
with believers in Damascus, the disciples in
Jerusalem would have nothing whatsoever to do
with him. Acts 9:26 says, "On reaching
Jerusalem he made efforts to associate with the
disciples, and they were all afraid of him;
they did not believe he was a disciple."[5] Imagine
now, if you will, this remarkable thing. Ask
yourself this question: Why were they afraid of
Saul when he arrived on the scene after they
had heard the stories that had come down from
Damascus? The only reasonable explanation that my
mind conceives is that when they saw him there
was something about his outward appearance
and behavior that so put them off that everyone of
them rejected the possibility of his really
being a Christian. All except one of the disciples,
Barnabas, rejected him. His name meant
"Son of Encouragement." Mr. Great Heart
himself—Ole Barney. Could it be that after three
years of knowing Christ under the circumstances
that he had known him, there was yet so little outward
evidence that the disciples were afraid of him? To
me that seems to be the only reasonable explanation.
But true to his name, Barnabas looked
beyond the outward appearance and behavior, and
believed that Paul's conversion was real. He had
the courage to stand up for someone that everyone
else has rejected. But this is what Barnabas
did, and it was for this reason that the disciples
admitted Paul into fellowship. From Paul's account

in Galatians it would seem to have been a highly
limited fellowship at that. Remember now,
that Paul's first preaching experience in Damascus
had not exactly brought revival. It had brought a
riot, and it was because of that that they had had to
let Paul over the wall in a basket in order to get
him safely away into the Arabian desert.

It is Paul himself who admits in Galatians that
on his first visit he stayed in Jerusalem
only fifteen days. However, for one reason or
another, he omits telling why his visit there was
cut so short. Luke tells us why in Acts 9:28-30.
Paul preached in the Greek-speaking synagogue in
Jerusalem, and brought forth the same violent
reaction from his hearers. They sought to
kill him. I don't know about you, but if my first
efforts at preaching had brought two such
responses as that, I would have been so discouraged
in my soul, I don't think I would ever have
preached again. However, such was not to be the
case in the life of Paul. The Bible indicates
that after only fifteen days in Jerusalem, when the
disciples there learned of the plot to kill
Paul, "They conducted him to Caesarea and sent
him off to Tarsus."[6] Paul's comment in Galatians is,
"Afterward I went into the regions of Syria
and of Cilicia; but I remained personally unknown
to the Christian churches of Judea. They
only got it from hearsay, 'Our erstwhile persecutor
now preaches the faith he once laid waste.' "[7]
To get to Tarsus one has to go through
both Syria and Cilicia. It's understandable that
Paul would not want to remember some of the
specific humiliations that he received in the
cause of Christ. But Luke, that careful
historian, in the verse directly after the one indicating
that they sent Paul home, uses these almost

insulting words; *"Then* indeed the church
enjoyed peace all over Judea, Galilee, and Samaria,
strengthened within and progressing in reverence
of the Lord. And through the encouragement
of the Holy Spirit there was increase in
numbers."[8] What seems to be implied is that when
the trouble maker went home a revival broke
out. I realize that one could push that too far, but
it is an interesting succession of events to
speculate on. In the period directly after that, there
is no mention of the Apostle Paul through
the remainder of Acts 9, 10, and only at the very
end of chapter 11—verse 25—is there another
mention of the Apostle Paul. In Paul's account in
Galatians he clearly indicates in chapter 2,
verse 1, that it was some fourteen years later that
he got back to Jerusalem again. He remained
in Tarsus for that entire time. We have
no way of knowing what kind of ministry he had
there from the way the narrative of his life
is picked up in Acts 11:25. It states that Barnabas,
now ministering in Antioch in Syria, makes a
trip to Tarsus to look for Saul, and on finding
him brings him back to Antioch where he companied
with them for an entire year. According to
Luke, the second visit to Jerusalem by Saul took
place when he and Barnabas went to take the
money which the Christians in Antioch had
collected in order to meet the famine-caused needs
of the Christians in Judea.[9] Saul is not mentioned by
name again until chapter 12, verse 25, when it
indicates that Barnabas and Saul returned from
Jerusalem when they had finished their ministry there
and brought along John, surnamed Mark. It was
after this that the Holy Spirit said, "Set me
apart Barnabas and Saul for the work to which I
have called them. Then, after fasting and prayer and

laying on of hands, they sent them away. So then, they were sent out by the Holy Spirit."[10]

According to this then, the gap between Paul's conversion and his separation to a specific heavy responsibility was in the neighborhood of eighteen years. Three years in Damascus and the Arabian Desert, fifteen days in Jerusalem on the first trip, fourteen years in Tarsus, and a year in Antioch during which time he made his second visit to Jerusalem. That adds up to eighteen years, or thereabouts, before the heavy responsibility of ordination was laid upon Paul.

I shrink inside when I think of the times I have mounted the pulpit, recited the conversion experience of the Apostle Paul, and then indicated that he went out and turned the world upside down for Jesus Christ *immediately*. This simply was not the case. There is difference of opinion among scholars concerning New Testament dating. But it seems rather plain that many years went by before the Holy Spirit laid the dramatic burden on Paul as a missionary of the cross.

I do not for one moment mean to imply that Paul was not busily engaged witnessing for Christ all the way through this period of time. However, at least in the early years his effectiveness as a communicator was somewhat less than a spectacular success, according to the Bible. Undoubtedly, it was out of his own personal experience that Paul said to the young pastor Timothy, "Lay hands of ordination on no one hastily."[11] Paul knew quite well that it had taken him years and years to reach a point of maturity that could bear responsibility. The blunders that the church has made in violating this biblical admonition are too numerous to catalogue.

What I'm pleading for is that all of us see

ENEMY

that it takes a long time to bring a spiritual infant
with a tiny beachhead to a point of reasonable
maturity. Paul's life is an example for all of the
unlimited patience of God. Let's rejoice in it, let's
bathe in it, let's comfort ourselves in it. Let's
be patient with one another as we're in
this process of growing. It's painful for all of us to
face ourselves and get in touch with painful data
and put it under the domination of the Holy
Spirit. I do not, for one minute, intend to
condone evil within us. God knows, and I know,
that I would like to be done with all of the
evil within me right now. But let's face it, that just
doesn't seem to be God's way. I remember
another memorable quote from my friend
Manford Gutzke as he was relating the zeal that
he knew as a new Christian. Then he enrolled
in a Bible college and took a course in Church
History. He said, "That's when I realized
that God didn't seem to be in much of a hurry. That
being the case, instead of rushing off to the
mission field I decided that there was time for me
to get a good sound education!" If ever
there was a place where the old axiom, "Haste makes
waste,"[12] is true, it's in the care and feeding of newborn Christians.

When I was a kid and growing my first row
of vegetables or flowers, I had the philosophy
that if a little fertilizer was good, a lot was
better. Much to my dismay, I discovered that I
had burned up my young plants. Fertilizer
actually increases growth to the point where a plant
literally burns itself out trying to use up all of
the food it has been given. I honestly feel that
we in the church have frequently been guilty of the
very same thing. There is nothing which we
need more than a sense of pace in bringing
young Christians along. I think we need this sense
of pace with ourselves, as well as with others.
Somehow, we have got to make our approach
to Christian education based more on one's spiritual
age than on one's physical age. A thirty-five-year-
old babe in Christ who is put into a Sunday
school class that is considering predestination and
election is probably going to get a little more
fertilizer than he can use.

It's interesting that in our day we consider
that a young man is old enough to go off and fight
a war if he is eighteen years of age. I know
that I was a lieutenant junior grade with all of
my combat experience behind me before I was
twenty-one years of age. I wonder if perhaps what
Paul's life really tells us is that it takes just about
as long to grow from a beachhead baby to
reasonable spiritual maturity as it does to grow
to a young man or a young woman. Could it
not be that Paul had this in mind when he
said, "But we were gentle among you as a mother
feeding and caring for her own children. We
loved you dearly—so dearly that we gave not
only God's message but our own lives too."[13]

So many of us have been led to believe that
maturity comes rather rapidly, that when it

doesn't appear in us we become covered with guilt
and quite certain that only we are plagued with
the problem of slow spiritual development.
As I have brought the essence of this message to
various gatherings of ministers and Christian
workers all over the world, it has warmed my heart
to see the comfort that it has brought. I think
of the young man in Melbourne, Australia,

who came to me after hearing this message and
broke down in tears. For just awhile, I held
him in my arms, much as you would a baby. When
he dried his eyes, he related the following story:
He had been converted to Christ in a zealous,
evangelical church. He had learned all the
right things to say, all the right responses to give,
and had excelled in verbal expression and in
observing the right "don'ts" of behavior. His minister
urged him to go right into Bible school. This he
did after knowing Christ for only a year. He
was so outstanding in his academics at Bible
school that they asked him to remain as an instructor.
He was fully equipped and could make all of the
right sounds and express all of the seemingly
right attitudes. Yet, inside he was spiritually a
frightened little boy. He realized how spiritually
young he was in point of time. He also came to
see how dreadfully unfair he had been to himself, in
making severe judgments about his absence
of inner maturity.

I'm not suggesting we wait eighteen years to ordain
people to ministry, but rather that we learn to
gauge maturity by Bible standards. We must
allow enough time for individuals to mature before
saddling them with heavy responsibilities.

When my daughter, Susie, first went to school
I remember on one of my visits there seeing a
little boy about six years old whose eyes were

brimming with tears and whose chin was
beginning to quiver. You could see he was
terrified. His father took one look at him and in a
very stern and severe tone said, "Be a man!" The
one thing a six-year-old boy can't be is a man.
No way. He's a six-year-old boy, and he has a right
to be frightened at the prospect of all the
strangeness of school. Yet, for centuries this is what
we have been shouting at our feeble little babes
in Christ. Worse yet, we teach them to shout
it at themselves. No wonder so many live under
constant burden of guilt and self-accusation. It
takes time, time, time, and Paul's life is an
outstanding example of this. How good, though,
that his life also exhibits the unlimited patience
of a loving heavenly Father.

At one point in World War II, my squadron had
ridden out from Pearl Harbor to Saipan on a
British aircraft carrier. When we arrived, our ship
was nowhere in sight, so we were dropped on
the beach to live in tents until our ship did show
up. The enemy had been driven back into the
hills, but we could still hear the thump of
artillery fire from our position on the beach.

As was often the case in situations like that,
our troops set up for the showing of movies
in spite of the fact that the enemy was so near at hand.
There were three positions for movies on the
beach.

One night at one of the showings, some rather
unusual high-pitched laughter was noticed by
a member of the shore patrol. Upon investigation
he discovered two enemy soldiers sitting there
loudly enjoying our Mickey Mouse movies. It
was evident that they had run out of food up
in the mountains, had slipped through our
lines, stolen food and—what else would you

do after dinner?—were taking in a show. Such audacity! The enemy watching our Mickey Mouse movies!

I'm embarrassed to say that spiritually speaking, the same experience has been mine more times than I like to admit. In areas I had long since dedicated to Jesus Christ, I have detected the enemy carefully observing some of my Mickey Mouse fantasies. When and if it happens to you, just know that you have lots of company, and do to your enemy what the shore patrol did to ours that night. They hauled them out of there—they didn't even let them finish watching the cartoon!

What comfort to know that I'm not the only one it has taken a long time to get better. I'm in good company—no less a man than the Apostle Paul. "So comfort and encourage each other with this news."[14]

Spiritual maturity does not come automatically with the mere passage of years any more than physical maturity does. Life is sustained and growth is accomplished by good health habits— daily intake of good food and exercise. The same pattern must be observed to sustain spiritual life and growth. The food is the Bible[15] and exercising in godliness is hard work.[16]

> *The heights by great men reached and kept*
> *Were not attained by sudden flight,*
> *But they, while their companions slept,*
> *Were toiling upward in the night.*[17]

10

Too Much Too Soon

IN THE MOVIE *Dr. Zhivago* there is a
scene that is both horrible and instructive.
It is a gorgeous summer day and the Communist
forces, who are involved in the overthrow
of the czar, have taken up a position just in the
edge of a thick forest. From the vantage point of
the deep shade and the heavy growth, they
are lined up on their horses looking out over a
sundrenched open meadow. As the camera moves out
across this meadow with its waving grass, one
can see in the shimmering distance a troop of
the czar's soldiers marching across the field in
perfect order. Their loose-fitting white uniforms are
in stark contrast to the nondescript clothing of
the revolutionaries.

As the czar's troops move closer and closer,
one of the revolutionaries lifts up his rifle and
begins to take aim. The commander of the
Communist forces indicates that he is not ready for
firing to commence. Closer and closer the troops
march, directly into the ambush that is set for
them. Finally, when the troops are well within range,
the commander slowly lifts his rifle and takes
aim, followed by all of the other soldiers, and firing
commences. The first barrage decimates the
ranks of the czar's force. The others let out a cry
and begin to run instead of dropping into the
protective cover of the tall grass. What follows is
almost as though the revolutionaries were
observing target practice on humans. None of the
czar's troops can outdistance the guns leveled at
them. When the last soldier is down, the
firing ceases.

Now, the Communist forces ride slowly out to
make certain that their handiwork is complete.
As they near the scene of the carnage, several of

them dismount. As they approach the first
prostrate forms, a bewildering childlike cry is heard,
"Mama! Oh, Mama! Mama!" Quickly the
revolutionary leader rolls over the first form from
which the cries are coming, and discovers there,
not a soldier but a young boy of about nine or
ten years of age. In rapid succession other forms
are examined, and the oldest of these soldiers
would not exceed eleven or twelve years of age.
Only the leader of the troop was a full-grown
man, and even the hardened Communists are
revolted by the idea that he would have led these
children into battle.

It is a scene of sickening horror, but I wonder
if it is not possible that the church has been,
over the years, guilty of the same thing. If, indeed, it
does take years to arrive at a level of spiritual
maturity able to bear responsibility, and I
think it does, then is it not possible that we have
been dressing up spiritual children in the uniform of
the King of kings and sending them out against an
adversary for whom they were no match? All
one has to do is look at the list of ministers
demitting the ministry and Christian workers going
into secular jobs to begin to realize that it may
well be true. Add to that the number of
missionaries sent out who have been shattered
under the pressure of too much too soon, and the
picture we see is not one of which the church
can be rightly proud. "Lay hands on no man
suddenly."[1] This is a biblical warning that we have
failed to heed, and the ineffectiveness of many
churches can be traced directly to the haste with
which men have been ordained, both as
ministers and as lay leaders, such as elders, deacons,
stewards or vestrymen. Any of us who have
been in on the organization of brand new

churches have seen bewildered men elected to high office with no training and little qualification other than the fact that they were present. The truth of the matter is that one's spiritual condition is not nearly so important to the electing group as one's secular position. If a man is a leader in the community, it is automatically assumed he will, therefore, be a good leader in the church.

There have been those occasions where unregenerate men have been elected to the highest office that the church proffers simply because they were men of influence and affluence in the community. The fact that they might be spiritual infants didn't even enter into the thinking of those who proposed their names and assisted their election. 1 Timothy 3:10 suggests that church officers first prove themselves before they are elected and ordained.

As tragic as all of this is, there is yet another category of Christians for whom my heart bleeds even more. That is, the simple babe in Christ who is placed in a church context where, with no regard to his spiritual age, he is compelled to assume positions of responsibility long, long before he is ready. My own early days in the church saw many blunders, not the least of which was teaching people to traffic in unfelt truth— demanding expressions of the gospel in a verbal way that could not possibly be matched in the inner recesses of the heart. These people were too new to the Christian faith. I thank God for those persons who resisted successfully my effort to clap a mold on them that demanded too much too soon. I am ashamed of the attrition rate that took place among those who simply could not bear the pressure of performing beyond their experience, and so drifted away from all contact with

me or the church. I grant you, it could be that
some of them were just not truly converted
to Christ, but there also would be a large segment
of them who were, but who could not bear to
participate in the hypocrisy that was being thrust
upon them. If only I could have seen then what I see
now. But lest I curl myself up in a big ball of
guilt, I have to remember that I was afflicted by
teaching that never really came to grips with the
importance of pace and patience in bringing
the Christian along slowly, but surely, to a point of
maturity. I suppose part of it could also be
blamed on the fact that I was too much involved
in my own spiritual babyhood to be able to do
much more than deal with the incessant
crises that seemed to be plaguing my own existence.

When we continue to put people beyond their
depth in the Christian life, the strain involved
robs that life of the essential joy that one should
know in following Jesus Christ. Among the most
tragic developments of all has been the
tendency in the church to take those of us with
bizarre backgrounds and make us overnight sensations
on the evangelical testimony circuit. I don't
doubt the sincere motivation of those who vault
spiritual babies into national prominence
overnight. I'm sure they are quite proud of the
work of grace that God has wrought in a human
heart. But few of these people can handle this kind of
heavy publicity when they are so spiritually immature.

Donald Allen was a young man who had
everything going for him. Gifted with a plus
personality and rugged good looks, he was the idol of
his high school. Outstanding in athletics and
with the physique of a Greek god, he seemed to
have the world at his feet.

A devil-may-care attitude, however, combined

with a constant urge to demonstrate his manliness
proved his undoing. Three times expelled from
high school for drunkenness and unruly conduct he had finally hit the skids to a completely
desolate life of debauchery. Arrested several
times, he became the talk of the small town in which
he lived. Neighborhood wags would shake their
heads over him and whisper the latest gossip
concerning his escapades.

It was at this low point in his life when he hit the
skids that God stepped into his life. Converted
during a special evangelistic campaign in a local
church, his climb out of the gutter was even
more startling than his descent had been. Invited
to give his testimony the Sunday following his
conversion he proved to be an effective public speaker.
Seven accepted Christ as a result of his testimony.
Invited to other churches to give his testimony
to the grace of God he soon found himself in
great demand as a speaker. Within two months he
was holding his first evangelistic campaign with
many more churches and religious organizations
demanding his time. He seemed to be skyrocketing
to the very pinnacle of Christian service.

A whirlwind courtship with a wonderful and
gifted Christian musician seemed only to
enhance his value as an evangelist. His wife played
the marimba with exceptional ability. Together
they seemed an ideal team. Then criticism
began to come his way. This, combined with the
fact he was not mature enough for the responsibilities
of marriage, had a decidedly unsettling effect
upon him. He became more and more remorseful
and withdrawn in himself, often sitting in his
room for hours and refusing to speak to anyone,
even his wife.

Donald having no foundation under his crisis

conversion, seemed unable to understand that
the Christian life was intended to be a slow
but steady growth in the grace and knowledge of the
Lord Jesus Christ. The very fact that it had
proved to be no bed of roses seemed to leave him
bewildered. Still serving the Lord today as a
pastor, his whole Christian life has been one of abrupt
change and departure whenever criticism came his
way—often leaving a church without a
moment's notice. He regrets greatly today the
fact that he was shoved into Christian service so
fast after his conversion. His usefulness for the
cause of Christ has been greatly diminished because
he lacked the spiritual maturity necessary for
the demands made upon his time and talent.

It would appear that the worse a person has
been in his pre-Christian days the more likely it is that
he will be made into an overnight celebrity
because misguided Christians expect too much
too soon. When the overnight Christian
hero finally falls on his face, these very ones who
encouraged him into getting his mouth so
far out in front of his life will be the first to have
nothing to do with him. With clucking tongue and
under-the-breath condemnation this dear
collapsed brother will be condemned for the
dishonor he has brought on the gospel. Granted that
every individual is responsible for the person
he becomes, there is yet gigantic responsibility
that must be borne by those who send spiritual infants to do the work of the mature.

Such was the case of Brett Carson with a
checkered past in prison and self-wrought disaster.
His conversion made him an overnight
sensation in his particular denomination. Encouraged by the leaders around him and because of
the natural glibness of his tongue he was soon set

up with his own evangelistic team and tent, traveling from pillar to post and startling people with the diversity of his preaching. To me he said, "The day that I walked outside my tent to admire my six huge, shiny trucks and two magnificent Cadillacs was the beginning of my downward plunge. I became so insecure in myself that at the beginning of many crusades I would go to the men's room in order to overhear the ego-inflating comments being passed there about me. This was a necessary part of getting sufficiently psyched up, and the reassurance I needed to get through the night!"

Needless to say, the downward plunge that began when this young man viewed all the magnificent acquisitions of his spiritual success, ended at the bottom. However, the wealth he now had made it possible for him to set himself up in a lucrative business that allowed him to continue his life in a movie star manner. It was only years later, at thirty-five years of age, that he began a contact with me, honestly searching for a way back to a normal relationship with the Lord that he loved.

Why does this happen? I believe it happens because few of us have yet to understand what to expect as a result of Christian conversion. I believe it happens because few of us understand how long it takes to move from spiritual infancy to that level of maturity that can bear responsibility.

For every spectacular conversion turned catastrophe that we know about there are thousands of ordinary people whose lives reflect the same kind of spiritual disaster. The cause is the same—a lack of understanding concerning what actually happens at conversion, and, more important, what yet has to happen.

There are so many more cases that could be cited. Like the one I know of personally: a vicious young gang member, converted to Christ and exposed on national television within a brief span of time after his conversion. As he was seen all over the nation, the invitations came flooding in from all over the evangelical world. There seems to be an insatiable appetite for the hearing and the rehearing of this kind of bizarre story. Encouraged by so many invitations, and overzealous Christians, he formed his own evangelistic association. Wherever he went, he did the very best that he knew how to do. However, slowly but surely, the invitations began to diminish. Finally he accepted an invitation to work with youth in a local church. It was only the kind and patient care given him by the pastor that sustained him through the sense of rejection that had developed because those who had helped to make him prominent no longer seemed to have a burning interest in him. After all, his story had been heard by too great an audience for a repeat, yet this seeming indifference and disaffection hurt. Through the guidance of the patient pastor, he is now really finding his gifts in a secular job, and doing Christian work on the side.

But the church's appetite for the sensational has not only a questionable effect upon the individual whose story is being used up and cast aside, it also has a bewildering impact on the simple believer who doesn't have that kind of a sensational testimony to offer.

Just how devastating an impact this has on the nonsensational believer was illustrated for me in the comment I heard a man make to a friend as we were leaving a meeting where a sensational testimony had just been offered. His

words made me shudder! What the man had said was
not offered in bitterness or complaint, but, rather,
with a tone akin to wishfulness. He said it
during the coffeebreak at a luxurious retreat
center. What he said was his way of reacting to a
testimony we'd all just heard. The person
testifying had been one of those weird
Christian phenomenons called "a boy preacher."

After ordination at a ridiculously young
age, this man had become an alcoholic, left his
wife and kids, tried to kill himself, ended up
in a mental institution, and there had
emerged into a fullblown trust in Jesus Christ.
Through the love of Jesus and his new life in the
Holy Spirit, he had been restored to sanity,
reconciled to wife and children, and had
found a new fulfilling vocation outside of the ministry. It was a stunning testimony concerning the
power of our Savior, and during the coffeebreak
everyone was buzzing about it.

Now, about those words that made
me shudder—the plaintive words of the man
who was listening to everyone else rave
about the "great testimony." What he said was,
"Sometimes I wish I had been bad enough
to make it on to some Christian program for
a testimony!"

Understand, I can shudder over those words
without in any way detracting from the
marvel of what Jesus our Lord had done
for the testifier. I shuddered because of the
startling truth revealed about us evangelicals
in those words. A sordid past is almost
required if one is to fit into the category of
"great testimonies." We lionize and make
celebrities of people who have been
lifted out of the gutter of sin to a new life

in Jesus. Understand me, please! I praise
God for the power of Jesus to accomplish this, but
I believe the time has come for us to soberly consider what we are doing to all believers by this
tendency to exalt a prurient past. The most obvious
impact is on the average believer like the man who
uttered those words. Never a spectacular sinner,
he observed that what Jesus had done for him
didn't seem important enough to other Christians
to have him share his new life in Christ.

How often I have heard people say to me,
"I don't have much of a testimony. You see, I was
raised in a Christian home, and have always
loved Jesus, studied my Bible, gone to church, and
tried to witness in my own way."

Let's face it! That's the most glorious kind
of testimony to have. Glorious, because the
life has not been sullied by the grosser sins, nor the
body wounded by satanic violations of it.
Yet, we evangelicals have almost made a virtue out
of sin by our celebratizing those of us who have
wallowed in it prior to our conversion. It makes
one wonder if perhaps there isn't some sort of
an insidious vicarious enjoyment which the Christian
experiences in hearing a recitation of all of
another person's previous sins.

Another true story illustrates my point. A
beautiful young model had been led to Christ
by my wife. After a very brief period of time
she dropped by my study and ran off a rather
stunning list of invitations that she had to give her
testimony. Her testimony included a well
publicized divorce with all manner of immoral
accusations hurled around in the proceedings that
made good reading copy. When I evidenced
something less than gigantic enthusiasm over this list
of appearances for her, she asked me why. I asked

her to answer a question for me. I said to her,
"If you were just a plain Jane who was not a
photographic model, do you think you would
have received these invitations to speak?"

"No," she said slowly, "I guess if I were just
plain Jane, they would not have invited me."

I then asked her another question, "Would plain
Jane's experience of Jesus Christ be any less
valid than yours?"

Again, she responded, "No, I'm sure it wouldn't
be!"

Then I said, "Do you suppose that what they
are secretly interested in is your past life more
than your present life, because that's the only
difference between you and a plain Jane who has
found Jesus Christ?"

I could see that my words stunned her, and it
took her awhile to answer, but then she said,
"Why, why. . .that's just awful."

"Yes," I said, "but the worse part of it is
that these people are not in any way aware of what
they are doing, either to you or to the plain Janes
who sit in the audience and wonder why no
one ever invites them to give a public witness."

One of the things totally overlooked in reference
to the "sensational testimony" that bespeaks
a sordid background is the on-going impact that the
sordid background has on the believer. Let me
illustrate. Any way you look at it, Jacob was a
cunning character, a deceiver, and, in some
ways, a coward. It was not until he struggled with
the angel of God that his nature was so changed
and he got the new name of Israel. But the
Bible indicates that Jacob limped away from that
encounter, and limped all the rest of his life.

My background would hardly fit under the
category of sordidness that some have experienced,

but it was bad enough for me to be glad that God
has forgotten about it. I only wish I could.
There is a real sense in which I have limped
psychologically and emotionally because of those
patterns of misbehavior that characterized my
early life. Like Jacob, we have a new nature and a
new name, but there is still enough of the old
nature on hand to create a limp. There are
scars. I know that I am forgiven in all eternity for
these things. Yet, there are temporal consequences that I must live with the rest of my life.

Let me illustrate further. Here is an unmarried
girl who is pregnant, and the young man who
helped her get in that condition has shown his
true colors by fleeing the scene. There is no way
she can win in this situation. If she gets an
abortion, her conscience is stuck with this for the
rest of her life. If she has the baby and puts
it out for adoption, she forever wonders where the
baby is, who it's living with, whether it is being
treated right, or if it is even healthy. Every time
she sees a child of that age, she's struck with
a memory. Moreover, if she keeps the child, she
and the child are then saddled with the perpetual
reminder of the illegitimacy. Say in the course
of the unwanted pregnancy and in the utter
loneliness of it all, she comes to the saving
knowledge of Jesus Christ—she knows that her sins
are forgiven. Yet, there is a real sense in which
she lives with the temporal consequence
forever, regardless of which course she takes.
Frequently, in the Christian world in our facile
evangelical excitement over bizarre backgrounds, we
will not even allow this kind of person to
verbalize or face up to their psychological and
emotional scars in our dogmatic insistence that in
Christ all things are new. In view of the fact that

our enemy-held islands are never totally conquered by God's forces on this side of Glory, we continue to suffer at least part of the consequences of past misbehavior.

Even as I say this, I want to plead guilty to my own charge. I have become so used to this pattern of operation that I almost do it without thinking. When I do think about it, I don't do it. I suppose you can say I'm reduced now to pleading with my readers to prayerfully, carefully, consider the impact, either of expecting too much too soon of the babe in Christ, or of turning those with bizarre backgrounds into overnight celebrities. This makes them overnight Christian leaders who simply do not have the spiritual maturity to proceed for very long without causing gigantic disappointment to many who have been led to look up to them. We must avoid exploitation at all costs. The price paid by everyone is just too high.

11

Child Prodigies?

IN EVERY AREA of art and academic discipline, history has recorded a few child prodigies. Television shows have been built around some of them who had amassed a gigantic amount of information at a very early age. Others have had mathematical skills that were mind boggling to say the least, particularly to those of us who find it difficult to balance a checkbook. At no point did anyone suggest a revision of education and its curriculum in order to provide a challenge to the exceptional. Only in recent days have there been those classes where exceptionally talented children could proceed at a faster rate than the rank and file.

Yet, I do believe that a case could be made for the idea that the church has geared itself up in its educational processes for the spiritual child prodigy instead of the rank and file. The exception has been mistaken for the rule.

If you have plugged along with me this far, it is probably true that most of you have thought of some individual whose experience of Jesus Christ simply will not fit into the slow developing pattern of growth that has been outlined here. I'm sure that such people exist, although I do not now find it possible to recall to my mind anyone that would fit into the category of a spiritual child prodigy. There may be somebody that you know who fits into that sort of category. There have been people that I thought would fit, but when I got to know them better I discovered that they were having the same sort of slow-growing pains that I had. However, I do not deny the possibility that such people exist anymore than I deny the existence of the exceptional child prodigy in other realms of intellectual and artistic pursuit. As I look back in my ministry, I realize that a pattern developed for me. I tended to give far more time and attention to those people who started with a healthy beachhead and developed more rapidly than I did to those who may have started with a fragmentary beachhead and developed slowly. Not only that, I tended to judge the slow growers severely on the basis of those whose outward indication of growth was more rapid. Far be it from me to project my failures upon the whole Christian church, but I do believe I detect a trend in myself that is everywhere reflected in our attitude toward the rank and file Christian. We have based our whole doctrine of spiritual progress (sanctification) either on the child prodigy or upon those whose growth pattern was far more rapid than the average. I believe that one of the reasons why many pastors tend to become disillusioned about the long-range results of an evangelistic campaign is that they leveled a standard of judgment on the average new believer that should have been reserved for the occasional spiritual prodigy or his second cousin, the big beachhead more rapid growth believer.

In checking my dictionary[1] for a clear definition of the word *prodigy,* I was struck by the similarity of the root word for *prodigy* and the root word for *prodigal.* The word *prodigy* comes from a Latin noun, *prodigium,* which means "omen, monster." What is indicated by the root word is that the exceptional child with remarkable and outstanding abilities is a little bit on the monstrous side when compared with the normal. The root word for *prodigal* comes from the Latin *prodigus,* or *prodigere,* which means "to drive away," or "squander." I was first struck with the dramatic similarity of the two Latin words, although one is listed as a noun and the other an adjective. Then I was struck with another idea, which

I would not want to press too far. That is,
I wonder how many people have been driven out
into a life of prodigality because of the unreal
standard of a prodigy which has been applied to
all. In the intellectual realm, if the standard of a
prodigy was applied to the average person, it
would drive him into utter despair over the possibility of ever attaining to that level of intellectual
proficency. Is it not possible that we have
been doing the same thing in the spiritual realm?
As I said, I would not want to press it too far,
but it is something that is striking, and should at
least be given serious thought.

In a sense, what I'm doing is admitting that
there may be exceptions to the rule that I am suggesting in connection with the spiritual development
of Paul's life based on an understanding of
Christian conversion being like the invasion of an
enemy-held island, and that the Christian
maturation process is like the invading forces'
strategy and warfare to take that island. I admit
to the possibility of an exception, but I am begging
us to contemplate the possibility that we may have
made the exception into the rule.

While I was pastoring a church at Key Biscayne,
I walked one day along the beach with Billy
Graham, who was visiting me. I was greatly
burdened by my lack of spiritual progress and I
poured out my concerns to my friend. To illustrate
my point, I took a stick and drew a line in
the sand. First I drew an intersecting line
to indicate the time of my conversion to Christ. Then,
close to that line, I indicated a point to represent
where I felt I was that day in my Christian life.

In contrast, I marked a spot in the sand, far
off to the right, representing the spiritual perfection
which I so much longed to attain.

"Billy, why am I making such slow progress toward the place I feel God would have me be in my Christian growth? Why does the maturing take so long?"

Billy took the stick from my hand and marked a spot behind the point I had used to indicate "where I am today." "Lane," he said with characteristic graciousness, "if you are *there*, I am only *here*. The important thing to know is that the only hope for either one of us is that the gap between our achievement and the perfection of our Savior is covered by the blood of Christ."

Most of us are dreadfully embarrassed by the total failure of the twelve disciples after some three years of visible, physical companionship with the Lord Jesus Christ. Let's face it, their eyes had seen wonders that no human eyes had even seen before. Their ears had heard words like no other ears had ever heard, and their lives had been touched with the love and compassion that had never existed before the time of Jesus. Yet, when the chips were down, they failed him. One betrayed him, one denied him, and the rest deserted. I grant you that they had not yet received the Holy Spirit to give them the kind of courage that would turn cowards into conquerors, yet they had experienced Jesus Christ in the flesh in ways that most of us envy. Anyway you look at it, their development was slow. I remember one of my seminary professors telling me that after the resurrection of the Lord Jesus and the infilling of the Holy Spirit on the day of Pentecost, God finally had to resort to persecution in order to drive the disciples out of Jerusalem so that they would begin to fulfill his Great Commission. Although I believe that God is sovereign, I would rather attribute that persecution to the wickedness of men.

The delay in getting about the Great Commission was part of God's plan. He was waiting for them to mature to the point where they could shoulder the responsibility.

Evangelicals traditionally have been somewhat embarrassed by a late dating of the New Testament documents. Yet, if some of us love John's Gospel the best, could it not be that it was written from the vantage point of some sixty years of experience with the living Christ and with certain insights about the person and work of Christ that only mature reflection could have given him? When you see the love that exudes from the pen of this "son of thunder," one can only assume a tremendous growth pattern from the time that Jesus gave him that appropriate nickname.

Perhaps you know some child prodigies in the Christian life. Wonderful! But let's not mistake the exception for the rule. Most of us run-of-the-mill Christians are slow growers. And the ground which the invading Spirit of God gains in our enemy-held island is a slow, tedious acquisition for his invading forces. I kind of think that God intended for us to enjoy the process. Yet, who could possibly enjoy the process when an unreal standard of development leaves him covered up with guilt and self-accusation?

What blessed relief came to me the day I realized for the first time that my lack of perfection was not a surprise to God at all. What overwhelming comfort came to me when I read these words of the Apostle John, penned some sixty years, at least, after the death and resurrection of our Lord Jesus. He said, "If we say that we have no sin, we are only fooling ourselves, and refusing to accept the truth. But if we confess our sins to him, he can be depended on to forgive us and to cleanse us from every wrong. (And it is perfectly proper for God to do this for us because Christ died to wash away our sins.) If we claim we have not sinned, we are lying and calling God a liar, for he says we have sinned. My little children, I am telling you this so that you will stay away from sin. But if you sin, there is Someone to plead for you before the Father. His name is Jesus Christ, the one who is all that is good and who pleases God completely. He is the one who took God's wrath against our sins upon himself, and brought us into fellowship with God; and he is the forgiveness for our sins, and not only ours but all the world's."[2] As I read those words I stared in almost shocked unbelief at something I had never seen before. That was the collective, personal pronoun "we." John was including himself in the company of those who continued to need the forgiveness of the Lord Jesus Christ.

Out loud I spoke as though to the Apostle in person and said, "Oh, John! Are you telling me that after three years of companionship with the Savior in the flesh and sixty years of being filled with the Holy Spirit and companionship with the Savior in his invisible state, you were still 'blowing it' and needing the forgiveness of the Lord Jesus Christ? John, John, when you say, 'We have an advocate with the Father,' does that really mean that you continued to that very day and hour to need the advocacy of the one who is the sacrifice for our sins?" When the full implication of what I had read dawned on me, tears of relief filled my eyes.

It has been hard learning to be happy with the process. It's so humiliating to be tripped up again and again on the same stupid failings. Yet, I can thoroughly identify these days with the old preacher who said, "Ah knows Ah ain't what Ah ought to be! But Ah also knows Ah ain't what Ah used to be! And Ah thanks God Ah ain't what Ah'm goin' to be!" That's the only posture I know of that gives me the capacity to be happy in the process.

12

Paul Finally Had Them All, but It Took Time

THUS FAR everything that we have said has pertained to the subject of the spiritual maturing process. We have discussed the invasion of a life by the Spirit of God and the internal Christian warfare necessary to bring maturity. The goal toward which we are moving is summed up in one word: *love*. What Jesus said is worth repeating, "By this shall all men know that you are my disciples, if you have love one toward another."[1] This kind of love is going to reveal itself in also producing a personality that is full of "joy, peace, patience, kindness, goodness, faithfulness, gentleness, and self-control."[2] That's the fruit of the Spirit which Paul called, "A still more excellent way."[3] The way that Paul spoke of is well illustrated in his glorious chapter on love—1 Corinthians 13. This is the fruit of the Spirit. The fruit of the Spirit should never be confused with the gifts of the Spirit.

We live in a day when the mere mention of the gifts of the Spirit arouses strong feelings and potential controversy. The very controversy that surrounds the whole idea of the gifts of the Holy Spirit which God gives denies the fruit of the Spirit in which those gifts must be exercised. Our most profound beliefs must be held and expressed in love or we add up to nothing.[4]

In the New Testament there are four lists of the gifts that the Holy Spirit brings: 1 Corinthians 12 and 14, Ephesians 4, Romans 12, and 1 Peter 4. Interestingly enough, each list of the gifts differs from the others. None are identical. The reason for the giving of these abilities by the Holy Spirit is found in Hebrews 2:4, "God always has shown us that these messages are true by signs and wonders and various miracles and by

giving certain special abilities from the Holy
Spirit to those who believe; yes, God has assigned
such gifts to each of us."[5] The second thing to see
is that the list of gifts is in reality God's worksheet
for his people. This is what God expects
us to do, and in order to accomplish his spiritual
purposes in this world, he promises to give us the
ability to do them.

It is my conviction that when the Holy Spirit
enters the believer's life at conversion, he
comes bringing the full potential of all his great
gifts. Some will be made evident very early
in the believer's experience—others may not become a reality until much later—some indeed may
never be drawn upon, but all the potential
is there, fully compatible with the believer's
temperament and talents.

I have labored the point that the development
of the fruit of the Spirit comes in a long,
drawn-out dynamic process. Doesn't it
just stand to reason that God would impart the
gifts of the Holy Spirit to us in the same sort of
long, drawn-out process? The absolutely marvelous
thing about receiving the gifts in a developmental
way is the fact that I'm never frozen in one position concerning the abilities that God gives to me. My
future can always be brighter than my past. All
one has to do is contrast the early life of Paul
with the later life of Paul to see that he had
not only developed the capacity to love, but had
received additional abilities along the way that made
him a far more proficient servant of Christ. I'm
sure that people are sincere when they insist that
everyone has received *a* gift, but I think we are
shortchanging ourselves when we say that, as
we shall shortly see. God has given me certain
abilities now that I did not have ten years ago, and

I trust that he's going to give me certain abilities in the future that I do not have right now.

Unfortunately, the Bible itself is frequently used as an excuse for the exercise of one gift. Over and over again, with monotonous sameness, I have heard an exposition of Ephesians 4:11-13 that runs after this fashion. God has given to each man (usually in this case, they mean clergyman) a gift. The gifts that are listed in Ephesians 4 are, the gift of an apostle, the gift of a prophet, the gift of an evangelist, the gift of a pastor, and the gift of being a teacher. Since the Bible indicates that the person who has the gift of being an apostle must be someone who has seen the resurrected Christ, we will say that under ordinary circumstances that gift is no longer being conferred in our day. In my acquaintance there is only one man that I know of who has had a visible manifestation of the reigning Christ. This came in his conversion experience and has not been repeated since then. The aim of God in conferring these gifts on people in the church is that ". . . .we all may arrive at the unity of faith and that understanding of the Son of God that *brings completeness of personality,* tending toward the measure of the stature of the fullness of Christ."[6] The question I would like to pose is this: Can we say a person is complete if his only interest is evangelism? Can we say a person is complete if his only interest is pastoral care? Can we say a person is complete if his only interest is prophecy? Can we say a person has a complete personality if his only interest is teaching those who have already been won to Christ by someone else?

Consider this. The man who wrote these words was an apostle, he was a prophet, he was an evangelist, he was a pastor, and he was also a superb teacher. At various points in his life and ministry, he exercised one of these gifts in priority to the others, but not to the exclusion of them. In other words, by the time Paul wrote this letter to the Ephesians, he had all of the gifts that he mentioned in this list in Ephesians 4.

However, when we come to the present day institutional scene we find this list of gifts most frequently offered as an excuse to exercise a ministry and manifest a personality that is something far short of being complete.

I remember hearing Bishop Jack Dain, of Australia, tell of his growing years in the church in England. One of his vicars maintained that he had the gift of a teacher, and all he did was to utilize his pulpit opportunities for teaching that was over the heads of most of the people, but sounding fantastically profound all the while. After him came a vicar who maintained that he had the gift of evangelism. His ministry included only evangelistic sermons and calling people to faith in Christ. Lest I seem to be blaming these men, whom I do not know, may I hasten to say that they were probably victimized by the teaching which they had received concerning the singularity of gifts offered by the Holy Spirit. A man got one gift and he worked it to death much to the utter despair of the people to whom he was ministering.

Another tragic development in our whole understanding of the gifts is involved in the institutionalizing of the church. Let me show you what I mean. If I say the word "evangelist," who pops into your mind? Billy Graham, of course. If I say the word "teacher," there automatically looms before our individual minds some person within our Christian experience whose profound teaching was a blessing to us. If I say the word "pastor," then the man who comes to mind is the person who cared for us and visited us when we were sick and sought us out when we were missing from the regular gatherings of the flock. You see, we only associate these gifts with people who are into the institutional framework and who carry labels with them that inevitably mark them as clergy.

When we put ourselves in the context of the kind of church that existed when these words were penned, and the kind of people that God had gifted as leadership, it's hard to marry our present day institutional image with that one. What I'm saying is that these gifts were not exclusively set aside for the clergy, but were offered to one and all. Moreover, I'm maintaining that these gifts were not offered in exclusion of the other gifts.

If a man involves himself in a life given both to studying and uttering of prophecy and has no concern for the broader spiritual condition of the people that he addresses, then I think he is eccentric. The evangelist who has no pastoral concern for the babes in Christ that come under his ministry is eccentric and not complete. The pastor who only pastors, and the teacher who only teaches without an evangelistic concern for those persons who never have made a commitment to Christ is far from being a complete personality. We must not limit these gifts to the clergy, nor must we ever contemplate exercising these gifts apart from a conscious awareness of the necessity of exercising these

other gifts. I spent nine years as an evangelist,
and during that period of time had a genuine concern
for the ministry that God gave me to my
fellow ministers, as well as a concern for what
happened to the babes in Christ after they had
made their commitment. My concern extended
to what kind of teaching they would receive,
and whether they were aware of the potential
of these days for the fulfillment of prophecy.

Perhaps the best illustration in my own life
of the necessity of the multiple expression of these
gifts came when I was conducting a Crusade
in Christchurch, New Zealand. During the time
of the Crusade when I preached to thousands of people, I had to exercise the gift of the evangelist.
The ministers in the churches of Christchurch
had invited me to conduct a city-wide campaign for
the purpose of evangelism.

I then tried to sneak in a one-day vacation to
Mt. Cook in the Southern Alps of New
Zealand. In the seat behind me on the plane
was a middle-aged American lady who constantly
badgered me concerning what we were seeing
out of the window. I knew little more than she
did about the scenery outside, but, to satisfy
her and amuse myself, I made up logical
names for a lot of what I saw and offered them
as explanations concerning the view. I deplaned
at my appointed destination in the Alps, but
she remained on the airplane.

When I arrived in my motel room, my phone
was ringing. It was the director of the
School of Evangelism being held in Auckland,
New Zealand. The school was being offered
in conjunction with the Billy Graham Crusade
that had just begun in that city. It
seems that I was to replace a couple of the

fellows who could not teach in the School, and it necessitated my immediate return to the small airfield to try and catch the next flight back to Christchurch and connect on to Auckland. I was placed on standby, and I was the last person to board the plane, and who did I sit next to on the flight back to Christchurch? Right! The lady who had so intruded herself into my flight coming up to the Alps. This time I realized that my being next to her was no accident. Quietly I prayed that God would tell me what the situation was and make me sensitive to meet her needs.

As I began to question her about where she came from, and got her attention off of the scenery, I found her quite ready to talk. When she found out that I was a Christian, she really began to open up. It seems that she had been forced by financial necessity to put her aging mother in a nursing home. When she did this, the mother accused her of killing her. After about a year in the nursing home, the mother died. But her daughter was absolutely covered up with guilt, feeling that perhaps she *was* guilty of killing her mother by putting her into a nursing home. It did not matter that there was no other way to do it and still support mother, she still felt guilty. I also discovered that this woman was a person who believed that Jesus Christ was her Lord and Savior.

I then pulled out my Bible and opened it to 1 John 1:9. I had her read the words slowly out loud. "But if we confess our sins, he is faithful and just to forgive us our sins, and to cleanse us from all unrighteousness."[7] I had her read it two or three times, and then accused her of having made a mistake. I

said to her, "I think you made a mistake in
reading that. It doesn't say that God forgives
you for all of your sins. It says *some*, doesn't it?"
She apologized, and then started to read it again.
When she got to that little word *all*, she stopped and
said, "No, it doesn't say *some* sin, it says
all." It was then that she sucked her breath
in in a sound near to a sob. "Oh! Oh! It says
ALL!" I then assured her that she knew
and I knew that she had not killed her mother,
but that she had simply been victimized by
the circumstances. "However," I said, "let's
just imagine that somehow you were guilty.
Do you suppose that 'all' that we read about
would include that guilt?" Her eyes now
brimming with tears, she said softly, "Oh, yes, yes,
yes!" I then took her to many other verses
in the Bible speaking of the complete forgiveness
of our Lord Jesus Christ.

When we deplaned in Christchurch, she took
one of my hands in both of hers, and said, "I
believe God put you on that plane to meet my need.
Thank you. Oh, thank you!"

I then rushed to catch the next flight to
Auckland, dashed out of the airport, leaped
into a cab, rushed to the scene of the School of
Evangelism, almost immediately moved into the
pulpit, opened the Bible, and began to
teach the students there what I've been trying
to share with you here. That is, that Paul,
by the time he wrote what we have in the New
Testament, was an evidence of a multiplicity
of the gifts that he said the Holy Spirit would bring.

Retrace my steps with me. In Christchurch
the *need* before me elicited the gift of evangelism
within me. On the airplane returning from the
Southern Alps, the need beside me drew out the

gift of the pastor within me. When I stood before ministers and seminarians in Auckland, the need before me elicited the gift of the teacher within me. Paul had all of the gifts of the Holy Spirit mentioned in Ephesians 4. In case you are reading along and muttering to yourself, "But he was the Apostle Paul, and I'm just plain me!" Then I hasten to say that it was Paul himself who said, "But I found mercy, so that to me, foremost, Jesus Christ might display his *unlimited patience,* to be an *example* to *all* who shall put their trust in him for life eternal."[8] Friend, if after many years of growth in the fruit of the Spirit, Paul had also grown to exercise most, if not all of the gifts of the Holy Spirit, then why should we continue to be incomplete personalities? Should we not aspire patiently to develop to "That understanding of the Son of God that brings completeness of personality, tending toward the measure of the stature of the fullness of Christ"?[9]

It might be well to face up to whether or not we really want a multiplicity of the gifts of the Holy Spirit. The reason is easy to see. If we receive these gifts, then we automatically have a responsibility to develop that kind of radar-like sensitivity to pick up the needs of people that God puts in our way, and then let that need draw from us the specific gift that is going to meet their need. It's a stretching experience, and certainly does increase one's work load. Needs that you could walk right by with indifference before begin to grab at your heart. By faith you try to meet that need.

We live in a day of "specialists," and this day has afflicted the church no less than any other discipline. There are medical men who are so highly specialized that they would

think it an insult to be asked to treat a
symptom that lies only six inches away from their
specialty. Lest we rush to condemn the
doctors, we Christians have become just as bad.

Obviously, it took Paul a long while to develop
this "completeness of personality" that
he writes about. It takes refined, Holy Spirit
sensitivity to respond to the real needs that
people often camouflage. All too often we
Christians spray our gifts on people
without being sensitive to the need that the person
really has. Let's don't be God's mouth to a
person who at that time needs you to be God's ear.
Don't be God's laugh to a person who at that
moment needs you to be God's tear. The fruit
of the Spirit represents the basic heart attitudes
in which the gifts must be exercised. Otherwise, the
best gifts become sounding brass and
clanging cymbal.

One of the dangers in both physical life and
spiritual life is that we often have an ability
before we have the maturity to properly use
it. For instance, humans are capable of
having babies before they are mature enough to
take care of them. They have the ability
to procreate but not the maturity to offer the
proper parental care. This frequently seems to be
the case in the spiritual realm as well.
We somehow receive the ability to share
our faith in Jesus Christ before we have developed
the maturity to really care for the spiritual
baby that our gift may bring.

A friend of mine said the other day, "Isn't
it nice that God arranged it so that a woman
could not have a baby more frequently
than every nine months?" What he was hinting
at was the possibility that there might be very

great advantage in Christians not being able to have more spiritual children than they had the time to take care of. I've often wondered what would happen if we evangelists really assumed the responsibility of the care and feeding of every spiritual baby we brought into the world. It would be my opinion that Billy Graham has probably done more to try to accomplish this through well-trained counselors and alert churches than any other evangelist in history. Yet, one of the frustrations that all of us had in those days when I was on the Graham Team was the lackadaisical attitude of the average church member toward really becoming a guardian angel to the people they had counseled in the Crusade.

Since we have already established Paul's life as an example to all of us who have come to believe in Christ, maybe we should look at his sensitivity and concern for his infant believers. This is what he said to a group of them, "But we were as gentle among you as a mother feeding and caring for her own children. We loved you dearly—so dearly that we gave you not only God's message, but our own lives too."[10] He was not only a prophet, he was an evangelist. He was not only an evangelist, he was a pastor. He was not only a pastor, he was also a teacher. It took time—a long time—but finally Paul had them all. Remember, too, that the Savior that Paul served also represented every one of those gifts as well. Since we are to be "conformed to the image of God's Son,"[11] perhaps the goal for which we should strive is the same one that brought Paul completeness of personality.

13

The Hardest Place to Win the Battle— at Home!

"**I** WILL TRY to walk a blameless path, but how I need your help, especially in my own home, where I long to act as I should."[1] I identify with those honest and straightforward words of the Psalmist.

A number of years ago there was a popular song whose words reflected the negative side of what the Psalmist said. It went like this: "You always hurt the one you love, the one you shouldn't hurt at all. You always take the sweetest rose and crush until the petals fall." It is a sad irony that this is so frequently true. Out of ego needs, we put our best foot forward for the people we care the least about, and our worst foot forward for the people who mean the most to us. The old Pennsylvania Dutch saying, "Vee iss too soon oldt, and too late schmartt!" certainly applies to this writer. It has taken me a long time to catch on to what I was doing to my family, and even longer to catch on to the reason for it.

I honestly believe that the hardest place in the world to live out your faith in a mature way is in your home. It is relatively easy to fake out the people on the outside and give the distinct impression that you are an utterly mature person. It is at the core of your life, in your home, where the presence or absence of genuine Christian love makes itself known. I am impressed that much that I have learned over the years has been learned the hard way and at great personal sacrifice on the part of those nearest and dearest to me. I'm sharing these hard-gained insights about relationship in the home because I sincerely believe that this is where the measure of maturity must finally be taken.

The invading force of God in our enemy-held islands has got to make his presence known in this part of our lives, or we are just deluding ourselves. Many a minister's wife suffers in agonized silence over the hypocritical gap between her husband's "pulpit-posture-of-perfection" and the childish, ego-ridden man she has to live with at home. The same can be said for the wife and children of many lay leaders in the church as well. After the Sunday show at the church, the halo begins to slip askew, and if the leader is thwarted by the mate, the halo breaks in two and becomes horns. In my own case, I compounded that horror by suggesting that anyone who thwarted the great "man of God" at any point was surely an emissary from the devil himself. Surely not everyone is as dense or dull of hearing as I was, but the frequency with which one discovers unhappiness in Christian homes indicates a need to return to the Bible and take a second look at what it suggests as the basis for a Christian marriage.

In the last 25 to 30 years, we have seen an unprecedented flood tide of topflight help for family life. Videos, radio programs, seminars, retreats, countless books and tape recordings cover every aspect of Christian family life. The difference between men and women, the importance of deep-level communication, the solutions to sexual adjustments, the meaning of body language and every other conceivable aspect of marriage and the family has been explored in detail. Most of it has biblical backup, and some of it relates the best in psychology to each situation. (Some is awkward application of "pop psychology," albeit offered with a sincere desire to help the home situation.) This help extends into an A-to-Z coverage of raising children, plus a similar flood tide of wonderfully produced, up-to-the-minute, state-of-the-art materials for children. Every difficulty, from sex to senility, is dealt with in constructive and helpful ways. Good counsel is at every hand, and the church has made its people aware of its availability. Camps, conferences, tours, retreats, stadium rallies and even cruises are offered to help the Christian family. In one of my pastorates I started a Christian Psychological Center to meet these needs with highly trained and certified psychologists. It was immediately flooded with clients, and its growth was nothing short of phenomenal.

I commend these efforts to uphold the integrity of the family. I, myself, have been helped by much of what is available, and frankly, I don't feel I can improve on it. *Yet during that same time, the divorce rate among Christians has gone up to such an extent that it is little different than the divorce rate in the rest of society.* Divorce among the clergy during this period has increased alarmingly as well. Some statisticians have suggested that, in some areas, the rate of divorce among clergy has risen above that within the congregations. Given the wonderful helps available to us, what can we say to these statistics? One positive way to look at it would be to speculate on how horrible the family breakups would be had it not been for all of this assistance.

However, I suggest that we may be overlooking something so fundamental, so simple, so foundational that its omission is the reason the rest of the help is not solving the problems. As a matter of fact, the solution is so basic that I'm almost afraid to bring it up lest you slam this book shut, insulted by what you may think is a "given" for Christians. I beg you, don't do that. Hear me out! To introduce this radical suggestion to you gradually, let me slip up on your blind side by telling you two stories out of my own experience.

I didn't know how many people to expect. Although nearly 3,000 were registered for the Congress on the Bible II, I was just one among nearly 30 seminar leaders. The roster of those seminar leaders read like the "Who's Who" of

Christendom. I figured they had included me in the list so they'd have one "Who's That?" in the midst of the "Who's Who." I worried that no one would come to my seminar. However, they had given me a great subject to teach on: "How to Strengthen Your Marriage." I was floored when over 200 people came. Obviously, it was the subject that pulled them in, evidencing the epidemic need in the home.

I had asked for a setup of round tables with ten people at each table. On an overhead projector, I had placed a hand-printed, homemade copy of the Ten Commandments. After introducing myself and offering a prayer, we dimmed the lights and I illuminated the Ten Commandments on the screen behind me. There was an audible response from the audience when they saw what was before them. I could tell from the tone that their initial reaction was surprise at starting with something that seemed so unrelated to the subject of "Strengthening Your Marriage." While they looked on, I read the commandments aloud.

I then announced, "You've got exactly ten minutes to discuss at each table this question: 'Which one of these commandments can you break without such disobedience having a negative effect on your marriage?' Appoint a spokesman to report your decision to the whole group at the end of the ten minutes." I repeated the question for discussion and said, "Start now!" After a bit of mumbling, the room fell silent as one and all stared at the screen, going through the commandments one at a time, lost in thought. Then slowly, one by one, they turned back to face each other across the table and begin their discussion. The longer they talked the louder the noise level rose in the room. Finally, I called, "Time."

I repeated the question: "Which one of the Ten

Commandments can you break without it having a negative effect on your marriage? Table number one, what's your answer?"

"None," their spokesman said. He added, "It's unanimous!"

"Table number two?"

"None! And, it's unanimous!"

"Three?"

"The same!"

"Four?"

"None!" And so it went all around the room. Not one dissenting vote! It amazed me. Put five Presbyterians in a room, and you'll end up with at least ten opinions on anything. I know. I "are" one! Yet here was this large group of people in total agreement in their answer to the question.

I then asked for a show of hands for another question. "How many of you had premarital counseling with a Christian clergy person or counselor before your wedding?" About forty percent of those in the seminar raised their hands. I then posed a follow-up question: "In the counseling you received from a Christian clergy person, how many of your counselors ever brought up the Ten Commandments as being relevant to marital happiness?" Not one person raised a hand.

I then asked, "How many of you have had post-marital counseling from a Christian counselor?" About forty percent of the group responded with upraised hands. I then asked, "In your post-marital counseling, how many of you had your counselor bring up the Ten Commandments as being relevant to marital happiness?" Again, in the silence, not one person raised a hand. I then said, "In the light of what you've decided about the relevance of the Ten Commandments to marital happiness, how does this make you feel?" A middle-aged man jumped to his feet and said, "It makes me mad as can be! It was the breaking of those commandments that destroyed my marriage. If I had been clearly forewarned of this, the woman I still love might yet be my wife!"

Bear with me while I tell you one more story to make a shocking point.

I was speaking at a national gathering of youth leaders for high school evangelism of one of the largest evangelistic organizations in the world. Once again, I began my presentation with a question, asking for a show of hands.

"How many of you, after leading a high school student to Christ, teach them the Ten Commandments within the first year of their walk with Christ?" Not one hand was raised!

Next question: "How many of you will teach that same student the Ten Commandments in the second year?" Answer: None!

"Third year?" None! The truth was that they never taught them the Ten Commandments.

I then said, "This is a rhetorical question. I don't want to embarrass any of you. How many of you can recite the Ten Commandments and get them in the right order? They wouldn't have to be exactly word for word, just so long as you remembered the main idea of the commandment."

The next morning one of the most mature, long-serving women in this organization came up to me. "Last night," she said, "I took four of our bright young ladies with me to the condominium where we are staying. I sat them down and asked, 'Do you know the Ten Commandments, and can you recite them in order since Lane said the order was important?'" She said to me in quiet shock, "Can you believe it took five of us two hours to finally agree that we had all of the commandments? When we turned to Exodus 20, we discovered that, indeed, we had named all ten of the commandments, but we did not have them in the right order! You can be sure that all of us have taken on the responsibility to memorize them and teach them to the kids we lead to Christ!"

This chapter is about the family, and I want to jump right in and show you the amazing thing about these fantastic commandments. But first, I must convince Christians in America that the Ten Commandments are still in force, not relegated to the past as a failed means of achieving our salvation. The commandments were never given as a means of achieving salvation, but were given *after* salvation had been bestowed on the Israelites in Egypt. They were saved from slavery in Egypt through their faith in the word of God concerning the efficacy of the blood of the Passover Lamb. *After* they were delivered from Egypt, God led them to Mount Sinai, where he gave them the law. The motive for obeying the commandments was to be gratitude for that deliverance. The prologue should always be repeated before quoting any or all of the commandments. It says, "I am the LORD your God, who brought you out of Egypt, out of the land of slavery."[2] Implied by that statement is the word, "Therefore." Or, "since I have saved and delivered you, in gratitude, 'You shall have no other gods before Me.'" That he never expected them to be able to keep those commandments perfectly is confirmed by the fact that he *then* gave them the tabernacle and the animal sacrificial system as a means of conferring external forgiveness.

What was the Old Covenant (Old Testament)? Listen to the words of Deuteronomy 4:12–13: "Then the LORD spoke to you out of the fire. You heard the sound of words but saw no form; there was only a voice. *He declared to you his covenant, the Ten*

Commandments, which he commanded you to follow and then wrote them on two stone tablets" (NIV).

What is the New Covenant? Listen to the words of Hebrews 8:6–10 and 13 (NIV): "But the ministry Jesus has received is as superior to theirs [the Old Testament priests] as the covenant of which he is mediator is superior to the old one, and it is founded on better promises.

"For if there had been nothing wrong with that first covenant, no place would have been sought for another. But God found fault with the people and said: 'The time is coming, declares the Lord, when I will make a new covenant with the house of Israel and with the house of Judah. It will not be like the covenant I made with their forefathers when I took them by the hand to lead them out of Egypt, because they did not remain faithful to my covenant, and I turned away from them, declares the Lord.

"'This is the covenant I will make with the house of Israel after that time, declares the Lord. *I will put my laws in their minds and write them on their hearts.* I will be their God, and they will be my people.' . . .

"By calling this covenant 'new,' he has made the first one obsolete; and what is obsolete and aging will soon disappear." (This is a direct quote in the New Testament that comes, word for word, from a prophecy in the Old Testament in Jeremiah 31:31–33.) Since God has put his law in our minds and in our hearts in the New Covenant, what is obsolete and aging and will soon disappear is the sacrificial system, temple worship and all the dietary laws, not the moral law of God. In the New Covenant, a "new place" is found for the Ten Commandments. They come off the tablets of stone and are now written in the mind and in the heart. The law of God, then, is at the heart of the New Covenant.

A number of covenants were mentioned in the Old Testament. How do we know for certain which one he had in mind? Notice the reference to the covenant that God made with Israel when he "took them by the hand to lead them out of Egypt." It is, then, the covenant of the commandments that he refers to. God confirms this in Hebrews 10, quoting the important part of the Jeremiah prophecy again.

Some of you might be saying, "What about the Scripture that says, 'We're not under law, but under grace'?" Well, get out your Bibles and read the whole verse. It says, "For sin shall not be your master, because you are not under law, but under grace."[3] How can you know what sin is unless you know exactly what the law demands? Sin is breaking the law of God, according to 1 John 3:4–6: "Everyone who sins breaks the law; in fact, sin is lawlessness. But you know that he appeared so that he might take away our sins. And in him is no sin. No one who lives in him keeps on sinning. No one who continues to sin has either seen him or known him" (NIV).

Still not convinced? You say, "What about Romans 10:4 (NIV), where it says, 'Christ is the end of the law so that there may be righteousness for everyone who believes'?" But the word translated there does not mean the law is banished or done away with. The root word, *telos,* means, "the final issue or result of a state or process," as in, "he is the complete fulfillment of the law." Christ is what the Ten Commandments look like lived out perfectly! Romans 8:29 says, "For those God foreknew he also predestined to be conformed to the likeness of his Son" (NIV). We cannot ignore the genius of the commandments that describe perfectly both the character of God, and the character of his Son. Is this not why the Son of God said in the beginning of the

Sermon on the Mount, "Do not think that I have come to abolish the Law or the Prophets; I have not come to abolish them but *to fulfill them*. I tell you the truth, until heaven and earth disappear, not the smallest letter, not the least stroke of a pen, will by any means disappear from the Law until everything is accomplished."[4]

I don't know where you are as you are reading this, but I sit with the most spectacular view of the heavens and the earth spread out beneath me and above me that you can imagine. It's all still here. And when you read the rest of the Sermon on the Mount, you'll see that our Savior expands the meaning of obedience to the commandments. He says that he not only wants outward obedience, but that he also wants inward attitudes to change as well. "But I tell you that anyone who looks at a woman lustfully has already committed adultery with her in his heart."[5] Honesty tells us that only Christ in me (and you) can possibly bring this inner change to pass. We can manage to control outward behaviors in our own strength to some extent, but when it comes to changing attitudes of hate, envy and lust, we plead, "God, be merciful to me, the sinner."

But now I want you to change gears completely. I want you to see that the giving of the commandments was one of the most splendid acts of the grace of God that the mind can imagine. Only the giving of the law incarnate in our Lord Jesus Christ exceeds it. At Mount Sinai, according to Psalm 103:7, God revealed both his character and his will to mankind. When he ordered us to be holy even as he is holy, he indicated that we would accomplish this by obedience to his commandments. And may I remind you that the Apostle John teaches us that his commandments are *"not burdensome."*[6] In 1 John 5:2–3, he states that we show our love for God by keeping his commandments, and that we show our love for the children of God by keeping his commandments. And doesn't it make sense that we show our love for ourselves by keeping his commandments? We can't do this in our own strength. God will give us his strength to bring this to pass.

If the heart and mind of the New Covenant is the Ten Commandments, doesn't this cry out for us to give close attention to those commandments? Is this

the possible missing foundation to all that good advice available to us regarding marriage and the home? If we don't begin our marriages by making these commandments the foundation of our relationship to one another, how can we possibly succeed, regardless of how good the advice is? Now, consider the simple question posed by the prophet Amos, "Can two walk together, except they be agreed?" You might well ask, "Agreed on what?" The answer: agreed that you are vowing, before God, your future mate and all witnesses to the marriage, that you have agreed on God's standard of right and wrong. And that you are promising him, and each other, that you are submitting yourselves to the authority of God, and that, relying upon his grace in Jesus, you intend to be held accountable to God's standard of right and wrong, both in what it forbids and what it affirms. You are thus making a contract with God, and one another, to live your life according to God's never changing standard of right and wrong. Remember what that group of over 200 people in Washington decided? They agreed that there was not one of these commandments you could break without it having a bad effect on your marriage.

If, then, breaking the commandments always has a bad effect on marriage and the family, then keeping the commandments, both in what they forbid *and* what they affirm, will always have a beneficial effect on the marriage and family. That's why it is so important to see that the commandments not only reveal the character of God and his will for man, but they comprise an amazing family contract.

I remember a huge government-sponsored Conference on the Family that was a disaster because they could never even agree on how to define "family." The conference broke up early without deciding anything. Had they looked into the Bible they would have discovered that the commandments define God's design for the family. It's simple: the "father" and "mother" are mentioned in the fifth commandment, and the "children" of that father and mother are mentioned in the second commandment. "Sons" and "daughters" are mentioned in the fourth commandment. They are implied in the fifth commandment, and implied again in the tenth commandment. This, then, is God's design for the ideal family—father, mother, and sons and daughters in the home. Period! Yes, there are families that do not fit this design, due to death, divorce or willful disobedience to God, but they are less than the ideal. Even pagan psychology and human experience confirm this. Not only do the commandments define God's concept of the family, they establish God as the only true source of authority for parents and, for that matter, any authority on earth.

Remember that God's law is the self-revelation of his character. God can be trusted to act toward us consistently with his character. Moreover, what pleases God is the same yesterday, today and forever. We surrender ourselves, submissively, to one who has revealed to us, in advance, precisely what he is like and how he will act in our behalf. (Anyone who submits, blindly, to undefined authority is a fool!) Now, consider how important this is for family life.

In the first four commandments, God establishes his authority over the entire creation, especially the pinnacle of his creation, mankind. When the father and mother are submissive to God's authority, the children can trust them to exercise that authority consistently. As you yield to God according to his law, your children will know how you can be trusted to act as soon as they know that law. They are yielding to well-defined authority. In her mid-teen years our daughter Susie went through some times of semi-rebellion. Later, having straightened out her life under the teaching of Charlie Riggs of the Billy Graham team, she confided in us, "Even in my most serious times of rebellion, I knew that what you were saying to me was right! I knew this because every morning the two of you started your day reading your Bibles and praying." She recognized our authority because she saw us submitting ourselves to God's authority, and she saw us doing our best to be obedient to that authority. This brings us to another terribly important biblical principle.

We have authority in the home only when our lives demonstrate that it is derived from being under the authority of God. All authority is derived from submission to a well-defined higher authority. The founding fathers of the United States understood this clearly. Read carefully the Declaration of Independence and you'll see. This is also why most state constitutions derive their authority to rule from God. When the Declaration of Independence was created, the only God spoken of was the God of the Bible. How do we know this? Because from the earliest times in this nation, people were sworn in for court testimony with their left hand on the Bible and their right hand raised. It was this written truth that was the standard for true testimony to be spoken. It was the God of this Book whom the witness looked to for the standard of right and wrong—for help in telling the truth.

The gigantic debate concerning who is the head of the household comes into a brand-new light with this understanding. Both father and mother are more concerned with their individual submission to the authority of God than with who gets the final say at home. Besides, if they're both submissive to the same standard of human behavior, almost all arguments will be resolved since both are marching to the same detailed instructions touching most of the important issues of life. "Can two walk together, except they be agreed?"[8]

Our Lord Jesus adds undeniable weight to this concept in Luke 7:1–10. That's the story of the Roman centurion who sends Jewish elders to our Lord, asking that his beloved sick servant be healed. As the Lord Jesus starts in the direction of the centurion's home, he is met by the centurion's friends with this message: "'Lord, don't trouble yourself, for I do not deserve to have you come under my roof. That is why I did not even consider myself worthy to come to you. But say the word, and my servant will be healed. For I myself am a man under authority, with soldiers under me. I tell this one, "Go," and he goes; and that one, "Come," and he comes. I say to my servant, "Do this," and he does it.'

"When Jesus heard this, he was amazed at him, and turning to the crowd following him, he said, 'I tell you, I have not found such great faith even in Israel.' Then the men who had been sent returned to the house and found the servant well" (NIV).

I have come to see that we cannot confer God's authority on another person. Nor does a family position or an ecclesiastical office bring God's authority with it. We only *have* God's authority when we submit to his well-defined authority.

Especially where the home structure is concerned, there is one more biblical dimension that must be dealt with. God's authority is demonstrated in family relationships only as moral authority. It cannot be coercive or demanding without violating the law of love. We confer moral authority on another person by voluntarily submitting to it. The entire church, as well as the home, needs to consider these shocking words of our Lord Jesus concerning the nature of true godly authority. The situation was this: James and John had been privately trying to set themselves up to occupy the number one and number two positions of authority with Christ in his coming Kingdom. When the other ten heard about this, they were indignant, probably wanting an individual chance at those positions for themselves.

Our Lord's response was enough to stop a runaway locomotive of ambition dead in its tracks! He said, "You know that those who are regarded as rulers of the Gentiles lord it over them, and their high officials exercise authority over them. Not so with you. Instead, whoever wants to become great among you must be your servant, and whoever wants to be first must be slave of all. For even the Son of Man did not come to be served, but to serve, and to give his life as a ransom for many."[9]

Do I hear some volunteers who wish to step forward as candidates to be "head of the household"? Now, concerning that place in Ephesians 5:22 that is so often quoted about who the head of the household is—are you ready to be a true servant leader? Most people I know would be delighted to submit to true servant leadership. What is there to fear from such well-defined moral authority as this? What is there to fear from a servant leader who has come, not to be served, but to serve and give his life for the one he serves? Do I hear some meek, male voices joining mine and quietly crying to the Lord Jesus, "Have mercy, dear Lord, have mercy"?

Three friends and I were resting between tennis games one day, having a high good time chewing up the elected President with harsh criticism. One of them said soberly, "I have to admit, I would not make a good President!" Then his face brightened and he blurted out triumphantly, "But I'd make a good king!" That's the average man's concept of "head of anything." But, a servant, a slave—just to be number one? Sorry friend, that's not my idea either. But, that's exactly what my Savior, and yours, says. That's what loving your wife as Christ loved the church means. That's what being willing to die for her means—dying to self, and living for Christ.

To understand the authority we're submitting to, let's look briefly at the first four commandments. Number one is simple. God demands absolute first place. He must truly be worth more to us than anything or anybody on earth. If he isn't, we don't truly "worth-ship" him. (Please, as you're reading this section, get out your Bible, turn to Exodus 20, and read the first 21 verses aloud. Then, as I move from one commandment to the next, reread that particular verse.)

Number two explains why we have so much trouble being obedient to the first commandment. Almost all of us have idols that we value more than God. Anything or anybody worth more to us than God is what we truly "worth-ship." The entire family is negatively affected by our violation of this commandment, even to the third and fourth generation. Obedience to this commandment sends blessings into thousands that follow us in the family line.

Commandment number three forbids that we

profess what we don't really possess. It means so much more than the verbal profaning of the name of God. To take God's name in vain means to take his name to no purpose. For instance, if we esteem something or somebody more than God, we are sinning when we profess to be true believers. When we take all of this partial commitment to church in "worship," we compound the problem in our mock observance of the Sabbath (commandment four).

Add to that our Savior's summary of these first four commandments and you see the humbling and desperate need we have for our Redeemer and Lord, Jesus. He said, "Love the Lord your God with all your heart and with all your soul and with all your mind."[10] Now we understand why the Publican, standing in the Temple next to the self-righteous Pharisee, beat on his chest, could not even lift his eyes to heaven, and cried out, "God, be merciful to me, the sinner."[11]

We'll be merciful in how we exercise the authority we have, seeing our own desperate need for mercy. "Blessed are the merciful: for they shall obtain mercy,"[12] our Savior said in the Beatitudes. To those critical of his association with sinful Matthew and his corrupt friends, he said, "But go and learn what this means: 'I desire mercy, not sacrifice.'"[13] He said to those critical of the few grains of wheat his disciples harvested and ate on the Sabbath, "If you had known what these words mean, 'I desire mercy, not sacrifice,' you would not have condemned the innocent."[14] This merciful attitude is to be shown mate to mate and parent to child.

Keep in mind that in the Temple, behind the thick veil, was the Holy of Holies, symbolizing the presence of the Holy God. In that sacred place was the ark of the covenant, and inside it were the tablets of stone on which God had inscribed his Ten

Commandments. But spread over the top of the holy law that brings such a searing conviction of sin, God himself had ordered that a golden mercy seat be placed. This mercy seat pointed toward that future time when the sacrifice of his only begotten Son would cause mercy to triumph over judgment.

Now, watch how beautifully the last six commandments unfold as the "Amazing Family Contract." The sequence of the commandments is crucial, as is recognizing the positive side of the commandments.

Having established the father and the mother (not the church, and surely not the state) as the surrogates for his authority on earth, God also indicates the family unit is the essential building block for society. In establishing the first family, God said, "For this reason a man will *leave* his father and mother and *be united* to his wife, and they will become *one flesh.*"[15] My wife and I became "one flesh" in a precious little blue-eyed girl named Susie. However, couples who have no children also become "one flesh" in the intimacy of sexual relations. In the mystery of childlessness, couples must learn to trust God with that destiny in the same way that couples with children face their task of parenting—by faith in the goodness of the will of God.

The sixth commandment teaches *respect for life:* "You shall not murder." I suggest to you that this commandment, for all its negative connotations, is actually a celebration of mother and father as co-creators with our Father in heaven producing a life designed to live forever. The presence of a newborn in the home is a wonderment beyond description. A baby boy or girl can force us to think about the most profound matters the mind can imagine. God doesn't deal in copies, only in originals. There was never a baby like this one before, and there will never be another like this as long as the world exists. Different down to his or her little fingertips, yet bone of our bone and flesh of our flesh. Designed by God to fulfill a destiny not like any other that will ever live. No wonder our Jewish friends joyfully sing, "To life, to life, La' Chaim!" We are to respect the wonder of life itself—your life, my life, the lives of countless others. We are to respect the life of the unborn, the aged and even the end of this earthly life. We do not will ourselves to be born, nor do we have the right to will ourselves to die.

And we are to respect the originality of other lives our Creator has placed on this earth. Loving our neighbor as we love ourselves surely has its beginning in this commandment. There is sanctity to life because we are created in the image and likeness of God.[16] Our Savior's summary of the last six commandments begins at this point: "'Love your neighbor as yourself.' All the Law and the Prophets hang on these two commandments."[17]

The seventh commandment teaches *respect for the sex act that brings life.* God, who invented sex, teaches us to respect such an invitation to become potential creators of *life.* Yes, the sexual act has a far broader meaning than just procreation, but none more profound. That potential alone justifies God's demand that sex be reserved for marriage between one man and one woman. Sex is the ultimate indication of trust and commitment. Its misuse is devastating society at this time in our history. There would be few abortions if respect for the act that can create life were the foundation of a man's and a woman's commitment to their God and to each other. Sexual faithfulness brings stability into the home as little else can. Obvious fidelity brings a great sense of security to their children as well.

This celebration and protection of the sexual act

also makes it obvious that this commandment forbids homosexual activity. Not only does such perverse activity have no chance of producing life, it has, instead, produced the most fearful and incurable epidemic of death the world has ever seen. Other passages in the Old and New Testament make this prohibition so plain that it is beyond interpretation or debate.

Remember what God says in Genesis about the man leaving his father and his mother and being united to his wife. This means that he must have another place than Dad's home for his fledgling family. How incredible that the eighth commandment teaches *respect for the private ownership of property.* When the commandment states, "You shall not steal,"[18] it assumes that you have the right to own property. The entire redemption story of the exodus from slavery in Egypt holds out the destination of "a land flowing with milk and honey."[19] Each member of each of the twelve tribes would own land on which to raise his family. This is essential for the well-being of the family since a man is to leave the home of his father and cleave to his wife. He needs a place to call home. When the founding fathers were debating the wording of the Declaration of Independence, many wanted this well-known part to read that, according to the laws of nature and of nature's God, we were entitled to certain unalienable rights, among which were Life, Liberty and *Property.* Where did they get such an idea? It came from the laws of nature and of nature's God—that is, the Ten Commandments.

In our early marriage, things got so tough for us financially that we retreated to Annette's home, and on another occasion to my parents' home. As nice as they were to do this for us, I burn with shame over it. It was wrong for our marriage, and in both instances, everything seemed to go wrong in our relationship. I felt less than a man at not being able to provide for my wife and for myself. Better to do with less and have your own place than to encroach on the home of others.

This commandment also establishes a fundamental economic principle that not only benefits the family but is essential for the well-being of society. This commandment defeats the communist/socialist concept of government ownership of property.

The ninth commandment is just as crucial to family well-being as the rest. It teaches *respect for the truth.* Annette and I have been married for over 51 years as I write this. I know of nothing more basic to marital happiness than love for the truth. Although the negative wording condemns false witnessing (lying), the positive aspect is love for the truth. The truth in this case is a person, our Lord Jesus Christ, who said, "I am . . . the truth."[20] He also said to God, "Your word is truth."[21] Continual study of the Word of God is called for to learn how he is the truth, and to learn the lessons of truth which he teaches in his written Word. But we must remember that this truth must be obeyed to be understood and appreciated. Jesus said, "If anyone chooses to do God's will, he will find out whether my teaching comes from God or whether I speak on my own."[22]

The more we saturate ourselves in his truth and the more we obey that truth, the easier it becomes to tell the truth in our family relationships. This is not only crucial between husband and wife, but also between parents and children, and children and parents, and children with one another. When we practice this at home, it becomes second nature to practice it outside the home as well. Falsehood destroys trust and relationships. In a society that rejects the idea of absolute truth, inevitably lying has become epidemic, reaching into the highest levels of government. Shamefully, it is reaching into the church as well.

The Bible's principles relate to the totality of human experience. This is truth not only for personal relationships but also for the reformation and transformation of the entire culture. The necessary foundation is the individual's commitment to and obedience to that truth in his relationship with God, his family, his vocation and his contact with the culture. The Great Commission indicates that the final aim is to transform nations through the reformation of their cultures. Our forefathers had that aim in forming the United States. We are called to embrace his truth in a determined effort to redeem our wayward society.

If you need any more convincing that these commandments constitute the amazing family contract, take a good look at the tenth commandment. This final commandment directs your attention away from your own family to your neighbor. "You shall not covet your neighbor's house. You shall not covet your neighbor's wife, or his manservant or maidservant, his ox or donkey, or anything that belongs to your neighbor."[23] Even as the commandments protect the integrity of your own home, your obedience to them protects the integrity of your neighbor's family and dwelling, and anything that your neighbor has. The positive side of this commandment calls for us to do everything within our power to enhance and protect everything and everybody that belongs to our neighbor's house.

Moreover, this tenth commandment proposes an economic truth that is desperately needed in today's political/economic dialogue. The eighth commandment establishes the God-given right to private ownership of property. In contrast, while the tenth commandment echoes that right for your neighbor as well, its wording establishes the possibility of inequality. Simply put, if your neighbor has prospered more than you have, with a better home and holdings, you have no right to covet (desire to acquire) what is his, nor to set about to get it from him. The positive side of this revelation shows that God in no way commands any state to indulge in the redistribution of wealth. You might even say that this commandment assumes that some will work harder, delay gratification longer, invest more wisely, save more prudently and be more generous stewards of God's material blessings. We are not merely forbidden from trying to take his property, but we are to rejoice in the fruit of his labors, do what we can to encourage him, and at the same time protect him in his endeavors. Stewardship involves an individual voluntarily redistributing his blessings according to God's biblical plan as he shares with those in need. Anyone or any government that punishes those who prosper honestly are directly violating this commandment. To the man who wanted our Lord Jesus to force what he considered an equitable division of an estate, the Savior said, "Man, who appointed me a judge or an arbiter between you?"[24] Then he said to his followers, "Watch out! Be on your guard against all kinds of greed; a man's life does not consist in the abundance of his possessions."[25] Equal opportunity was never meant to guarantee equal results.

Tragically, many of us get married without ever discussing the standard of right and wrong to which we both shall subscribe. Consider the vast array of matters covered when we dig into the law of God as the amazing family contract upon which we both agree. Think of how many problems related to raising our children we solve when they know that we are submissive to God's standards, and that we are holding them and ourselves to those standards.

Meditate on the kindness of God in sending our Savior to demonstrate what these laws look like in the most trying stresses a life can encounter. We can see in him the perfection of the law of God lived in total obedience—both to what it forbids and to what it affirms. God illustrated these commandments in the person of Jesus Christ. How overwhelming to watch him take the death we deserve for our rebellion. How completely melting to see his triumphant resurrection, bringing victory over our defeats. How exulting to consider that he would condescend to live in us by his Holy Spirit, so that we may be conformed to his image, learning to lead our families with a servant's heart.

14

Although We Continue to Be in the Battle, the War Has Already Been Won!

IT MAY WELL BE ASKED, "If the Christian life is the kind of struggle and internal warfare that you say it is, and if there is so much pain associated in dying to self, why even bother?" The answer is simple. Though the battles are a struggle, we know that the war has already been won. There's no chance that we can lose. Victory is sure and an accomplished fact. Moreover, right here while the struggle is going on, we do know the joy and love and peace and mercy and grace in that area of our lives that has come under the domination of the Holy Spirit.

Part of coming to reasonable maturity is discovering the truth so succinctly put by a friend of mine. He was a fairly new Christian and had come under the influence of his non-Christian friends, and while on a fishing trip had gotten pretty smashed on beer. When he arrived home in that condition, his wife took one look at him and locked him out and then phoned me. When I arrived, he was sound asleep in the back seat of his automobile. I drove him to the nearest motel, picked him up in my arms and carried him in and put him to bed. Just as I was brushing the sand off his feet, he woke up long enough to see his pastor cleaning him up for beddy-bye time. With a groan he plunged his head in the pillow saying, "Oh, no!"

The next day I went to see him. When it became apparent to him that in no way was I there to excoriate him for his misbehavior, he asked why. I said to him, "Because your conscience has been worked on by an expert, the Holy Spirit! You don't need any further punishment than what you've already given yourself. What you need now is to know that God has forgiven you, and today is the beginning of a whole new life for you."

He looked at me in relieved bewilderment, and made this classic statement, "I know I'm not what the Lord wants me to be, and I suspect I'm not what you want me to be, but I think you will both rejoice in the fact that you've taken all of the fun out of sin for me!"

When we come to that point in our lives, we begin to really know whose side we're on and begin to despise sin in ourselves. It's a struggle, but we can face what we really are because we know that victory is sure. The war has been won. It's hard to top this for an exciting announcement of that victory: "You were dead in sins, and your sinful desires were not yet cut away. Then he gave you a share in the very life of Christ for he forgave all your sins, and blotted out the charges proved against you, the list of his commandments which you have not obeyed. He took this list of sins and destroyed it by nailing it to Christ's cross. In this way God took away Satan's power to accuse you of sin, and God openly displayed to the whole world Christ's triumph at the cross where your sins were all taken away."[1]

Sure, we still have to face physical death, and for a reason: "Yet, even though Christ lives within you, your body will die because of sin; but your spirit will live for Christ has pardoned it."[2] The final obliteration of the last vestige of sin in your enemy-held island is accomplished by that physical death. But your spirit will live because Christ has pardoned it. You see, the sting has been taken out of that physical death because, "Death is swallowed up in victory. O death, where then is your victory? Where then your sting? For sin—the sting that causes death—will all be gone; and the law, which reveals our sins, will no longer be our judge. How we thank God for all this! It is he who makes us victorious through Jesus Christ our Lord! So, my dear brothers, since future victory is sure, be strong and steady, always abounding in the Lord's work, for you know that nothing you do for the Lord is ever wasted as it would be if there were no resurrection."[3]

This is why we can face that enemy-held part of our island with fearlessness. We know what's up ahead. We know already that the devil is the defeated enemy because of Calvary's cross. It's hard to beat this combination. What a combination! "The battle is the Lord's."[4] And we already know who has won the war. Even though you may be looking at a tiny beachhead in your life occupied by the Spirit of God, yet the promise is most certainly yours as it is to the most mature believer that between you and that heavenly future is the promised presence of Jesus Christ all the way. "And he guarantees right up to the end that you will be counted free from all sin and guilt on that day when he returns. God will surely do this for you, for he always does just what he says, and he is the one who invited you into this wonderful friendship with his Son, even Christ our Lord."[5]

With this kind of security, plus the knowledge of total forgiveness and Heaven assured, a question may be forming in the minds of some. It might go like this: "Well, if a person knows that he's already forgiven and has Heaven made, what's to keep him from going out and living any way he wants to?" I want to answer that by telling you a true story that happened to me.

I was conducting my first evangelistic meeting in a little country church in South Carolina. I gave an invitation for people to come and receive Jesus Christ one night, and about six people came

forward, among them a little boy twelve years old.
He was barefooted and poorly dressed. Later
the pastor told me that his mother was in a mental
institution and his father was a hopeless alcoholic.
In counseling with the lad, I said to him, "Son,
are your sins forgiven now that you have received
Jesus?"

"Yes, sir," he said.

"How do you know they are forgiven, son?"

"Because the Lord Jesus died for all my sins,"
was his response.

"You mean your past sins are forgiven?" I
queried. "What about your present sins, are
they forgiven?"

"Yes, sir, they're forgiven too."

Then I asked, "Well, son, you know that you're
not going to be perfect when you walk out of here.
What about your future sins? Are they forgiven too?"

"Yes, sir. They're forgiven too," he said.

"Well, then, if that's the case, what's to keep
you from walking out of here and living like the devil?"
I asked.

His response was classic. He said, "Well, sir, the
way I figure it, it was my sins what nailed him
to the cross in the first place. And I don't want
to cause him no more trouble than I already have."

You see, the boy's heart, now invaded by the
Holy Spirit, was expressing the gratitude that a
true believer knows, as well as the motivation that
anyone has who has seen what it cost God to
forgive him. The remembrance of that kind of
love can overpower strong temptation.

With that kind of victory assured and that kind
of Presence guaranteed, we can now face up to a
very important matter.

It has seemed to me in my Christian life that

I reached a certain stage of spiritual growth and literally longed and ached for more of God. I had a real God-hunger that led me to throw myself at almost any potential deepening experience of the Spirit of God. In spite of my efforts in this direction, the God-hunger remained. I since have come to see something I feel is very important. We can only go so far in our spiritual maturation process in seeking to know and receive the blessing of God directly from God himself. It is almost as though he brings us to a certain point and then steps back and says, "Dear, dear children, how brief are these moments before I must go away and leave you! Then, though you search for me, you cannot come to me. . . .and so I am giving a new commandment to you now— *love each other* just as much as I love you. *Your strong love for each other* will prove to the world that you are my disciples."[6]

When we focus on obtaining the power and affirmation of Christ exclusively from Christ himself we're overlooking the crucial horizontal relationships of love through which he always intended that we should both give and receive him and his love. "He that receiveth you, receiveth me."[7] I began to get that additional dimension that I longed for when I decided I would look for him in other people in whom he dwelt. The more I affirmed his presence in them, the more certainly I knew his presence and power in myself in a new and mysterious way. Since this is a rather new thing for me, I can only say that I'm tiptoeing on the edge of a brand new understanding of what it is to love my neighbor as I love myself. "Love the Lord your God with all your heart, soul and mind. This is the first and greatest commandment. The second most important is similar: Love your neighbor as much as you love yourself."[8]

This means that in order to learn to love my neighbor I have to learn what it is to really love myself. This is much easier said than done. What does the Bible teach about self-love? Well, as I see it, the essential nature of the love of God is found in Romans 5:8, "But God commendeth his love toward us in that while we were yet sinners, Christ died for us."[9] God's love is the kind of love that accepted me as I was, even when my behavior was reprehensible in the eyes of God. He didn't approve of my behavior, but he loved me and accepted me as I really was in spite of it.

As a prisoner once put it in a letter to me from jail, "Finally, as I see it, God doesn't change me in order to love me. He loves me in order to change me!" Love, then, is God accepting me just exactly as I am. That loving acceptance is, along with the Holy Spirit, the motivating power that gives me what I need to change my behavior. I no longer have to pretend to be something I'm not. Because of my security in the finished work of Jesus Christ I can be boldly honest about who I am and what I am like. I can face both my vices and my virtues. I can esteem the virtues and set about, by the mercy and power of God, to see his Spirit change the vices.

To love someone else, then, is to accept him as he is and not constantly be laying upon him a demand to change. It is this acceptance of the other person that begins to loosen up the channels of communication so that people can really reveal themselves to others and know others at the same level of self-revelation. My problem has always been a fear that if I really let you know what I am like, you wouldn't like me at all, much less love me. Consequently, most of us wear masks in order that people would not know exactly who we are. For that reason, we oftentimes pretend to be what we really are not.

The three leading psychologists who helped lead the way into today's helpful psychological disciplines were Freud, Jung, and Adler. Freud said man's greatest need was to be loved. Jung said man's greatest need was for security. Adler said that the greatest need of man was for significance. Interesting, that! Because it is usually in the pursuit of one of those three things that we put on a mask of pretense.

The other day I heard Keith Miller say, "Even if you really loved me, I probably won't believe it because I haven't really let you know who I am."[10] I'm not sure of your love unless I have shown the real me to you. This is often what causes one of the startling traps in romance and marriage. A guy sees a gal go bouncing by and says to himself, "Wow! I want that!" He knows that if he lets her know the very basic thing that he wants from her, she'll have nothing to do with him. So he's got to put on a mask. He puts his very best foot forward as the little gentleman, and begins to become to her the kind of person he feels she will respond to. It may not come anywhere close to resembling the real person inside. If she is attracted to him, the chances are she too will put her best foot forward and slip on a mask that she is sure will get a ring on her finger. After they are married and the masks begin to slip, each sees a stranger emerging from behind the countenance of the person they thought they knew well enough to marry.

In the pursuit of significance or in the pursuit of security we are apt to be outwardly what we must be in order to gain these goals. We pretend for so long that we lose touch with who we really are. Nathaniel Hawthorne once said, "No man can for any considerable time, wear one face to himself, and another to the multitude, without finally getting bewildered as to which is the true one."[11]

I'm not proposing that we indiscriminately rip our masks off and traumatize ourselves and everybody else by startling revelations. What I am suggesting is the possibility that we begin to search for that person who can be trusted to receive with Christian love our progressive revelation of self. I can bear this and he can bear this only when we are both operating on the basis of the security that is the gift of every believer in Jesus Christ.

There are two kinds of loneliness that grip us human beings. The first is an existential inner loneliness that only the Holy Spirit of God can fill in our lives. The second kind of loneliness is for another human being with whom we can have deep and honest relationships. Frequently, we get these things confused and look for some person to be to us what only God can be. If I'm hungry, it's no good to show me a steak dinner unless I can put the steak where the hunger is, inside of me. Our loneliness for God can only be alleviated when we are invaded by the Holy Spirit, and receive inner assurance of his perpetual companionship.

Just as frequently, we are looking for God to be to us what he always intended that another human being should be. Many are looking for manifestations of God in their own experience that would call for another incarnation on the part of Jesus. We will see him again, but not until the second coming. Until then he fully intended that each of us should be some reflection of his present incarnation in us, so that we could visibly manifest to one another that love and care, affirmation and concern that he desires that we sense from him.

Completeness of personality is our goal, becoming a well-rounded whole person manifesting at least in some vague reflection all of the aspects of the marvelous personality of Jesus. Perhaps the aspiration of trying to be like Jesus Christ is just too lofty to contemplate. But the Apostle Paul was a regulation flesh and blood human being. His life is an example for all—for you and for me and for all others who will come to believe in Jesus

Christ. And his life showed a healthy, strong, vertical relationship with God, and deep, abiding, and honest relationships with his friends. One has but to count the number of personal names mentioned in the 16th chapter of Romans to realize how deeply involved he was with other persons. Paul had it all. It took lots and lots of time. But as long as God gives us the time and shows us his unlimited patience, dare we settle for less than that completeness of personality which is the essence of maturity?

NOTES

CHAPTER ONE
1. 2 Corinthians 5:17 (KJV).
2. Galatians 5:22, 23a.

CHAPTER TWO
1. Revelation 3:20 (KJV).
2. John 14:17 (*The Living Bible*); Galatians 2:20 (TLB); 1 Corinthians 6:19 (TLB).
3. John 14:15, 16 (TLB).

CHAPTER THREE
1. Romans 7:15, *New Testament in Modern English* by J. B. Phillips. The MacMillan Co., New York, New York.
2. Isaiah 59:2, RSV, *Harper Study Bible*, Zondervan Publishing House, Grand Rapids, Michigan.
3. Revelation 3:20 (KJV).

CHAPTER FIVE
1. Hebrews 10:14 (TLB).
2. 1 Corinthians 1:8, 9 (TLB).
3. Mairet, Phillip. *Christian Essays in Psychology.* Published by Philosophical Library, New York, p. 61.
4. Ibid., p. 41.
5. Loc. cit.
6. Romans 7:15 (Phillips).
7. Hebrews 4:12 (TLB).
8. Hebrews 4:13 (TLB).
9. Romans 7:18 (TLB).
10. 1 Timothy 1:15, *The Holy Bible, Berkeley Version in Modern English*, Zondervan Publishing House.
11. Romans 7:23, 24 (Phillips).
12. Psalm 103:13, 14 (Berkeley).

CHAPTER SIX
1. John 15:3 (KJV).
2. 1 John 1:8, 9 (KJV).
3. 1 John 2:1 (KJV).
4. A portion of Chapter 6 appeared originally in *Decision* magazine as an article by Lane Adams entitled "Care of Newborn Christians." It was later reprinted as a pamphlet. This material is copyrighted © 1966 by the Billy Graham Evangelistic Association, and is adapted for use in this book with the permission of the Association.

CHAPTER SEVEN
1. Matthew 9:17 (TLB).
2. From a message delivered at the U.S. Congress on Evangelism in Minneapolis, Minnesota, 1966.
3. Philippians 3:11-14 (TLB).
4. Jeremiah 17:9 (Berkeley).
5. Mark 7:20-23 (Berkeley).

CHAPTER EIGHT
1. Matthew 6:33 (KJV).
2. Galatians 5:16, 17 (TLB).
3. Galatians 5:19-21 (TLB).
4. Romans 6:16 (TLB).
5. Colossians 2:16, 17, 20–23 (TLB).
6. John 13:35 (KJV).
7. John 13:17 (KJV).
8. Ecclesiastes 1:17, 18 (Berkeley).
9. Colossians 2:18, 19 (TLB).
10. 2 Corinthians 5:7 (Berkeley).
11. Luke 6:31 (KJV).
12. John 13:17 (KJV).
13. Matthew 4:4 (KJV).

CHAPTER NINE
1. 1 Timothy 1:15, 16 (Berkeley).
2. Galatians 1:16, 17 (Berkeley).
3. Galatians 1:18-20 (Berkeley).
4. Acts 9:23-25 (Berkeley).
5. Acts 9:26 (Berkeley).
6. Acts 9:30 (Berkeley).
7. Galatians 1:21-23 (Berkeley).
8. Acts 9:31 (Berkeley).
9. Acts 11:30.

10. Acts 13:2-4 (Berkeley).
11. 1 Timothy 5:22 (Berkeley).
12. Haywood, John. Proverbs, Part 1, Chapter 2, *Familiar Quotations by John Bartlett*, (Little and Brown).
13. 1 Thessalonians 2:7, 8 (TLB).
14. 1 Thessalonians 4:18 (TLB).
15. Matthew 4:4 and 1 Peter 2:2.
16. 1 Timothy 4:7, 8.
17. Longfellow, Henry Wadsworth. *The Courtship of Miles Standish, Familiar Quotations by John Bartlett* (Little and Brown).

CHAPTER TEN
1. 1 Timothy 5:22 (KJV).

CHAPTER ELEVEN
1. *Webster's Seventh New Collegiate Dictionary* (Springfield: G. & C. Merriam Company).
2. 1 John 1:8—2:2 (TLB).

CHAPTER TWELVE
1. John 13:35 (KJV).
2. Galatians 5:22, 23a *New American Standard Version*
3. 1 Corinthians 12:31 (KJV).
4. 1 Corinthians 13:3 (NASB).
5. Hebrews 2:4 (TLB).
6. Ephesians 4:13 (Berkeley).
7. 1 John 1:9 (KJV).
8. 1 Timothy 1:16 (Berkeley).
9. Ephesians 4:13 (Berkeley).
10. 1 Thessalonians 2:7, 8 (TLB).
11. Romans 8:29 (KJV).

CHAPTER THIRTEEN
1. Psalm 101:2 (TLB).
2. Exodus 20:2 (NIV).
3. Romans 6:14 (NIV).
4. Matthew 5:17–18 (NIV).
5. Matthew 5:28 (NIV).
6. 1 John 5:3 (NIV).
7. Amos 3:3 (KJV).
8. Amos 3:3 (KJV).
9. Mark 10:42–45 (NIV).
10. Matthew 22:37 (NIV).
11. Luke 18:13 (Berkeley).
12. Matthew 5:7 (KJV).
13. Matthew 9:13 (NIV).
14. Matthew 12:7 (NIV).
15. Genesis 2:24 (NIV).
16. Genesis 1:26–27.
17. Matthew 22:39–40 (NIV).
18. Exodus 20:15 (NIV).
19. Exodus 3:8 (KJV).
20. John 14:6 (NIV).
21. John 17:17 (NIV).
22. John 7:17 (NIV).
23. Exodus 20:17 (NIV).
24. Luke 12:14 (NIV).
25. Luke 12:15 (NIV).

CHAPTER FOURTEEN
1. Colossians 2:13-15 (TLB).
2. Romans 8:10 (TLB).
3. 1 Corinthians 15:54-58 (TLB).
4. 1 Samuel 17:47 (KJV).
5. 1 Corinthians 1:8, 9 (TLB).
6. John 13:33-35 (TLB).
7. Matthew 10:40 and John 13:20 (KJV).
8. Matthew 22:37-39 (TLB).
9. Romans 5:8 (KJV).
10. From a message delivered at the Celebration of New Life, First Presbyterian Church of Hollywood, California, February 1975.
11. Quoted by Robert J. McCracken in a sermon on the radio broadcast, "National Radio Pulpit."

Steps to Peace with God

 Step 1 God's Purpose:
Peace and Life

God loves you and wants you to experience peace and life—abundant and eternal.

The Bible Says . . .

"... we have peace with God through our Lord Jesus Christ." Romans 5:1

"For God so loved the world that He gave His only begotten Son, that whoever believes in Him should not perish but have everlasting life." John 3:16

"... I have come that they may have life, and that they may have it more abundantly." John 10:10b

Since God planned for us to have peace and the abundant life right now, why are most people not having this experience?

 Step 2 Our Problem:
Separation

God created us in His own image to have an abundant life. He did not make us as robots to automatically love and obey Him, but gave us a will and a freedom of choice.

We chose to disobey God and go our own willful way. We still make this choice today. This results in separation from God.

Our choice results in separation from God.

The Bible Says . . .

"For all have sinned and fall short of the glory of God." Romans 3:23

"For the wages of sin is death, but the gift of God is eternal life in Christ Jesus our Lord." Romans 6:23

Our Attempts

Through the ages, individuals have tried in many ways to bridge this gap . . . without success . . .

The Bible Says . . .

"There is a way that seems right to man, but in the end it leads to death." Proverbs 14:12

"But your iniquities have separated you from God; and your sins have hidden His face from you, so that He will not hear." Isaiah 59:2

There is only one remedy for this problem of separation.

Step 3 | God's Remedy: The Cross

Jesus Christ is the only answer to this problem. He died on the Cross and rose from the grave, paying the penalty for our sin and bridging the gap between God and people.

The Bible Says . . .

". . . God is on one side and all the people on the other side, and Christ Jesus, Himself man, is between them to bring them together . . ."
1 Timothy 2:5

"For Christ also has suffered once for sins, the just for the unjust, that He might bring us to God . . ." 1 Peter 3:18a

"But God demonstrates His own love for us in this: While we were still sinners, Christ died for us." Romans 5:8

God has provided the only way . . . we must make the choice . . .

Step 4 # Our Response: Receive Christ

We must trust Jesus Christ and receive Him by personal invitation.

The Bible Says . . .

"Behold, I stand at the door and knock. If anyone hears My voice and opens the door, I will come in to him and dine with him, and he with Me." Revelation 3:20

"But as many as received Him, to them He gave the right to become children of God, even to those who believe in His name." John 1:12

". . . if you confess with your mouth the Lord Jesus and believe in your heart that God has raised Him from the dead, you will be saved." Romans 10:9

Are you here . . . or here?

Is there any good reason why you cannot receive Jesus Christ right now?

How to receive Christ:

1. Admit your need (I am a sinner).
2. Be willing to turn from your sins (repent).
3. Believe that Jesus Christ died for you on the Cross and rose from the grave.
4. Through prayer, invite Jesus Christ to come in and control your life through the Holy Spirit. (Receive Him as Lord and Savior.)

What to Pray:

Dear Lord Jesus,

I know that I am a sinner and need Your forgiveness. I believe that You died for my sins. I want to turn from my sins. I now invite You to come into my heart and life. I want to trust and follow You as Lord and Savior.

In Jesus' name. Amen.

_____   _____
Date   Signature

God's Assurance:
His Word

If you prayed this prayer,
The Bible Says...

"For 'whoever calls upon the name of the Lord will be saved.'"
Romans 10:13

Did you sincerely ask Jesus Christ to come into your life? Where is He right now? What has He given you?

"For it is by grace you have been saved, through faith—and this is not from yourselves, it is the gift of God—not by works, so that no one can boast." **Ephesians 2:8,9**

The
Bible Says...

"He who has the Son has life; he who does not have the Son of God does not have life. These things I have written to you who believe in the name of the Son of God, that you may know that you have eternal life, and that you may continue to believe in the name of the Son of God." **1 John 5:12–13, NKJV**

Receiving Christ, we are born into God's family through the supernatural work of the Holy Spirit who indwells every believer...this is called regeneration or the "new birth."

This is just the beginning of a wonderful new life in Christ. To deepen this relationship you should:

1. Read your Bible every day to know Christ better.
2. Talk to God in prayer every day.
3. Tell others about Christ.
4. Worship, fellowship, and serve with other Christians in a church where Christ is preached.
5. As Christ's representative in a needy world, demonstrate your new life by your love and concern for others.

God bless you as you do.

Billy Graham

If you want further help in the decision you have made, write to:
Billy Graham Evangelistic Association P.O. Box 779, Minneapolis, Minnesota 55440-0779

Printed in the United States
25086LVS00001B/271-276

9 781594 671050